Successful Clay Pigeon Shooting

SUCCESSFUL

CLAY PIGEON
SHOOTING

Edited by Tony Hoare
Foreword by Keith Murray

The Crowood Press

First published in 1991 by
The Crowood Press Ltd
Gipsy Lane, Swindon
Wiltshire, SN2 6DQ

British Library Cataloguing in Publication Data

Hoare, Tony
   Successful clay pigeon shooting.
   1. Shooting (Field Sports)
   I. Title
   799.313

   ISBN   1 85223 566 7

Photographs by John Best.
Front cover photograph by Michael Black.

Throughout this book, 'he', 'him' and 'his' have been used as
neutral pronouns, intended to refer to both sexes.

Typeset by Taurus Graphics, Abingdon, Oxon
Printed and bound in Great Britain by BPCC Hazell Books,
Aylesbury

Contents

Foreword

I am delighted to write a short foreword to this book, which has been edited by Tony Hoare, a regular contributor to various clay shooting journals.

His choice of contributors in this volume is one which covers and represents all aspects of our clay shooting disciplines. Their ability to cut through the mass of technical information, without omitting or distorting the basics, makes this a book that shooters, expert and novice alike, will find enjoyable and easy to read.

Perhaps all our shooting will be the better for reading it, for the secrets of our leading performers are here revealed for all to study and emulate. The book might well be called 'Tips from the Top.' I am sure that it contains enough sound advice to

enable others to compete at the top level and become clay pigeon shooting champions of the future.

Keith Murray
Director,
The Clay Pigeon Shooting Association

Introduction

By Tony Hoare

Clay pigeon shooting has achieved phenomenal popularity in the last decade. It has more followers today than at any time in its 100-year history. Membership of the sport's governing body has more than trebled since the mid 1980s, and clay shooting's appeal is growing so quickly that it has become one of our most flourishing participant sports. It is estimated that up to 150,000 competitors take part in organized shoots each weekend.

There is an indescribable excitement and thrilling sense of achievement in reducing a flying clay target to dust. This, combined with the sport's inherent friendliness, attracts an ever-growing number of people every year. Some of them are content to participate purely for their own pleasure at one of the UK's many local shooting grounds. Other aspire to represent their country at one variation or another of the sport's three main disciplines: Sporting, trap or skeet.

As more and more shooters strive for recognition, the competition for international team places gets tougher every year. The intense will to achieve international recognition is clearly illustrated by the outstanding success of British shooters all over the world. Our team and individual performances regularly produce gold medals and in some disciplines, such as international sporting, British shooters are pre-eminent. They win regularly against the best from all the other shooting nations in every category, from juniors through to veterans.

Nowhere is clay shooting's growing popularity better illustrated than in the increasing number of entries received annually for our national domestic competitions, where even the rawest novice can test his skills against the finest competitors in the land. Each year sees new record entries achieved for events such as the British and English Open Sporting Championships, and competitions are being allocated more time annually to accommodate the increasing number of competitors.

It is a far cry from the 'straw bale' village shoot to the tension of a national or world championship, but, at whatever level shooters choose to perform, they share a common love of their sport and a profound appreciation of its rare qualities of camaraderie and healthy competition.

The comradeship in shooting is unique and often transcends rivalry. It is this

More people than ever are entering our national domestic championships.

remarkable fellowship which makes participation especially pleasurable – so never be surprised if you are performing badly and a person you are shooting *against* offers you the best-intentioned advice about why you are missing your targets!

It is regrettable that, despite the enormous popularity of shooting and our superlative success at international level, the sport rarely achieves satisfactory recognition in national newspapers. Sadly, the popular tabloid newspapers are usually more concerned with the negative aspects of shooting and firearms and largely ignore the positive ones which occur in competition – the prestigious international victories at home and abroad. I wonder, for instance,

how many people are aware that British shooters won fourteen medals – including three golds – at the last Commonwealth games in New Zealand?

On the Continent, the public has an entirely different attitude to shooting; the sport's champions are elevated to superstar status, as popular and instantly recognizable as international soccer stars.

This recognition occurs nowhere more than in Italy, the very heartland of fiercely competitive trap shooting. The experience of John Grice, who has written one of the chapters in this book, illustrates perfectly the Italian public's hero-worship of shooters. On the day in 1990 when John won his World Universal Trench title with an unprecedented performance in Italy, he was mobbed in the street by passers-by who had watched his outstanding victory against their favourites on live television!

We may not have live television coverage of competitions in this country, but we are fortunate in having a number of excellent magazines which do give appropriate prominence to clay shooting. They report the busy international scene as well as providing news on local clubs and also give comprehensive lists of forthcoming fixtures all over the country.

The fact that you are reading this book indicates that you already have an interest in clay shooting, but before we go any deeper into the sport's fascinating origins, and describe its thrilling disciplines and etiquette, a word of caution. Someone once said that every box of cartridges should bear the following health warning: 'The contents of this box are addictive!' Few of us take up clay shooting without becoming totally captivated. As you read on, it would be as well to remember that you have been warned!

National championships – a far cry from village shoots.

Two outstanding young FITASC shooters: Stuart Clarke . . .

. . . and Alistair Evans.

GLASS BALLS AND FEATHERS!

How did it start, this thrilling sport that now attracts so many followers, from literally every walk of life? Its origins are to be found in the sport of competitive live pigeon shooting, still very popular in some parts of Europe but banned in this country since 1921. Pigeons and even sparrows were specially caught and released from traps at the shooters command. The birds had to be shot within a defined distance of the trap.

However, there were considerable problems with this type of shooting. It was not always easy to provide the large numbers of birds required for a competition, and there were many attempts to find a suitable artificial target to replace them.

John Grice – mobbed by Italians.

One of the first solutions was glass balls filled with feathers but the problems caused by broken glass need no explanation here. Then an American called George Ligowski, from Ohio, invented the original clay pigeon target in 1880.

Clay target shooting soon became popular and attracted a large number of followers and, in 1892, the Inanimate Bird Shooting Association – the forerunner of today's Clay Pigeon Shooting Association (CPSA) – was formed. Their first competition was staged at Wimbledon Park, London, on 23 July 1893, and the sport became so fashionable and competitive that, in 1990, it was introduced into the Olympic games in Paris.

The CPSA as we know it was formed in 1928 and its growth in recent years has been exceptional. Its membership today is almost 30,000 and growing daily.

The eventual ban on live pigeon shooting in 1921 gave the sport an impetus which has continued to this day. However, the devices which throw the targets are called traps, the clays are usually referred to as birds and a target that is hit and broken by a shooter is a kill – just as in the days of live pigeon shooting.

Clays, which are not clay at all but a combination of lime and pitch, come in six sizes to simulate the flight of live quarry: standard, midi, mini, battue, rocket and rabbit. They are usually black, but other colours are available to enhance visibility against dark backgrounds.

The standard clay, which is four inches in diameter, is always used for trap and skeet shooting but organizers of sporting events may use combinations of all the clays to give shooters a greater variety of targets.

It is often the midi and battue which pose the greatest problems for shooters: the midi's flight is illusory – at 90mm it looks further away than it actually is and it

The clay targets: standard, midi and mini.

A battue.

A rabbit.

moves faster than a standard clay; the concave battue is erratic in flight, often presenting the shooter with a fast, dropping, edge-on target. Rockets, too, are deceptive in flight. They travel as fast as a standard clay but give the impression that they are moving slower.

THE CLAY DISCIPLINES

Clay shooting is divided into three main categories: trap, skeet and Sporting, although there are different disciplines within each of these.

A rocket.

There has been a large entry at this Sporting shoot, judging by the number of empty cartridge cases on the floor.

Trap Shooting

Trap shooting is derived directly from the sport of live pigeon shooting. The most basic of the trap disciplines is Down the Line (DTL), where five shooters standing in a line take it in turns to shoot at a going-away target. After taking five shots on one stand, the shooters move to their right, down the line, to shoot at another five targets. The sequence is usually completed when all the competitors have shot at twenty-five targets, five on each of the five stands.

Because the targets are relatively simple and not too fast, DTL is an ideal discipline in which novices can take their first tentative steps at clay shooting. It is also one where they can soon begin to record respectable scores – and there is nothing like breaking targets to encourage the beginner.

At the highest competition level, Down the Line demands intense concentration. One lost target out of 100 or even a second barrel kill, which does not score as highly as a target killed with the first barrel, can mean the difference between success and failure. Do not be misled by the apparent simplicity of the targets.

Another more difficult trap discipline is Automatic Ball Trap. In this, six shooters fire in turn at a single target which is considerably faster and far more angled than those thrown in Down the Line. The shooters fire once from each of five stands before moving to their right to shoot their next target and, once again, the sequence is completed when all the shooters have shot twenty-five targets.

Down the Line, the most basic of the trap disciplines.

The speed and wider angles of the targets makes Automatic Ball Trap more testing than Down the Line. It is especially popular in France where every other village seems to have its own layout.

Without doubt, the two most exacting Trap disciplines are Universal Trench and Olympic Trap, both of which demand absolute concentration and lightning reflexes. In Universal Trench, also known as Five Trap, very fast targets are thrown over a wide arc from five points in front of the shooter. Olympic Trap (or Trench), also known as Fifteen Trap, is widely considered to be the most difficult form of trap shooting and, as its name implies, it is an Olympic discipline. There are three traps in front of each of the five shooting positions throwing targets at widely differing angles and at speeds that can exceed 90 miles an hour.

Olympic Trap is especially popular in Italy, and Italian trap shooters tend to be the finest in the world. In fairness to British shooters, though, it should be pointed out that they do not have facilities for practice which begin to compare with the outstanding layouts found in many parts of Europe.

Bob Braithwaite, a vet from Carnforth, near Lancaster, won a gold medal for Britain at Olympic Trap in the 1968 Olympics in Mexico City and was awarded an MBE for his performance. For the record, Bob shot 198 targets out of 200 to win his gold – including 187 without a miss!

The fifteen traps used for Olympic Trench.

A new generation of trap shooters like Ian Peel and Kevin Gill, who were gold medallists in the 1990 Commonwealth games, are now blazing the international trail for Great Britain.

Skeet

Skeet evolved from a shooting game devised in the United States and was first known as Shooting round the Clock. Standard targets are thrown in a set sequence of singles and doubles from high and low trap houses and shot from seven shooting positions in a semi-circle. There is also an international version known as ISU Skeet, which is also an Olympic discipline. This includes an eighth shooting station between the trap houses, a mandatory gun-down position and an indeterminate delay of up

Blazing the trail for Great Britain, Ian Peel . . .

. . . and Kevin Gill.

Excelling at ISU Skeet, Ken Harman . . .

. . . and Andy Austin.

to three seconds during which time a legitimate target can be thrown.

ISU is an abbreviation for the International Shooting Union, the body which governs the Olympic clay disciplines as well as international rifle and pistol shooting. Because of the predictable trajectory of the targets, very high scores are not unusual in English and ISU Skeet, and concentration is again the name of the game in top-level competition, where British shooters like Ken Harman and Andy Austin excel at international level.

English Sporting

English Sporting is undoubtedly the most popular type of clay shooting. Its purpose is to simulate as closely as possible the flight of live gamebirds, and the description of targets at sporting shoots confirms

this. Walk around most sporting layouts and you will find targets on different shooting stands described as if they really were live quarry: springing teal, high pheasant, crossing pigeon, overhead duck, magpie and rabbit – all the targets one would expect to find in the field.

An imaginative shoot organizer can stage an enjoyable and challenging competition by using natural features such as trees and undulations in the ground.

Sporting is now so popular that more than 1,500 competitors are attracted every year to competitions like the British Open Sporting Championship, and many top competitors believe it is our shooters' grounding in English Sporting, a purely domestic discipline, that has given us such outstanding success at FITASC Sporting, the international sporting discipline. (FITASC is an abbreviation of the title of

All eyes on the high pheasant on this championship Sporting layout.

Waiting for a high bird at English Sporting.

the ruling body of the international version of Sporting, Federation de Tir aux Armes Sportives de Chasse.)

British shooters like A. J. Smith, John Bidwell and Mickey Rouse have swept all before them in world and European championships. Our women, too, are supreme performers on the FITASC circuit. Anthea Hillyer and Denise Eyre have won the world title an amazing nine times between them in recent years.

FITASC Sporting is explained in more detail later but, basically, competitors shoot twenty-five targets from three or four stands in squads of six shooters and, unlike in English Sporting, no two targets shot by any competitor are the same. It is the simulation of game shooting taken to the ultimate.

Because more trappers and traps are needed than for English Sporting, and much more time is involved in setting up a shoot – there are four layouts of twenty-five targets each for a 100-bird competition – FITASC is expensive to stage and

A. J. Smith – swept all before him in the world.

Waiting to shoot a driven bird in a big championship.

consequently shooters' entry fees are higher. Nevertheless, FITASC is growing in popularity and the impressive performances of British shooters in competitions all over the world has been truly amazing in recent years. As our shooters win world and European championships, their example is inspiring more people to try what many believe is undoubtedly the most satisfying form of clay shooting.

STARTING SHOOTING

It is likely that your first experience of clay shooting will be with friends at an informal local event, but if you catch the shooting bug and intend to compete seriously it is worth considering tuition from a qualified coach. You will find lessons advertised in the shooting magazines, and the Clay Pigeon Shooting Association publish a useful booklet listing qualified coaches in the various regions of the country.

Membership of the CPSA has many benefits for clay shooters and if you wish to take part in competitions at club, county, regional or national level is is really a must for an annual fee of only £20, or £15 for juniors.

Many competitions are registered events. This means that your score will be submitted by the shoot organizers to CPSA headquarters and you will be classified annually to shoot in a particular class in accordance with your level of ability based on the scores submitted.

The CPSA publishes a book of members' averages for eight disciplines every year and whenever you take part in a classified event you will be entered in the class indicated against your name in the averages book. At first you will probably be in C class, which means that if you entered a registered competition you would be shooting against other C-class competitors whose ability is similar to your own.

The advantage of this handicapping system is that although you may find yourself on a shooting stand with an AA-class shooter like George Digweed or Barry Simpson, you will not be in direct competition with him. And as you gain more experience and your scores in registered events improve, you will find yourself moving up through the classes.

Needless to say, not all of us have the ability to qualify for AA class – where average scores in registered Sporting events must be at least 75 per cent – but it is surprising what practice and regular competition can do for your scores.

The CPSA is recognized by the Sports Council as the governing body of clay shooting in England, and membership automatically gives you £2,000,000 public liability insurance cover while shooting. It also strengthens your case for possessing a

Shooters waiting their turn on an English Sporting layout.

shotgun certificate. Since the introduction of the Firearms (Amendment) Act 1988, a chief constable can refuse an application for a certificate if he is not satisfied that the applicant has 'good reason' for possessing a shotgun (*see* Appendix II). Examples of good reasons given in the Act are 'sporting or competition purposes'. It follows that membership of the body which governs competitive clay shooting is an advantage when you apply to the police for your certificate, although it is certainly not a guarantee that it will be granted.

Buying a Shotgun

Once you have your certificate, you will want to buy a shotgun and the type you choose depends on several factors. When

You may find yourself on a shooting stand with Barry Simpson.

you do decide to buy your first gun, you will be offered so much well-intentioned but conflicting advice that you will probably be totally confused. However, there are several basic requirements to bear in mind before you make your purchase.

The first thing to remember is *never* to buy a gun without trying it first. A gun that feels right for you in the shop can be a totally different animal once you start shooting with it – and if you have already paid out several hundred pounds it is a bit late to find out that it does not suit you. Many gunshops have arrangements with shooting grounds which allow you to shoot with a gun before you buy it, and most commercial shooting grounds sell guns and also have experienced coaches available to assist you in your selection.

It is most important that a gun fits you properly, which means that the stock, bend and cast are exactly right for you. Basically, the stock must not be too short or too long; too much bend (or drop) in the stock will result in the gun shooting low, and the cast will determine whether it shoots left or right. A good coach will be able to decide the best fit for you.

The type of gun you choose depends on the kind of shooting you expect to do. Design of guns varies for the different disciplines although there are multi-purpose shotguns available, which many beginners find ideal until they decide to concentrate on a particular discipline. The most common of these is the over-and-under multichoke, an all-purpose shotgun which can be used with great success at Sporting, Down the Line and other trap disciplines as well as Skeet.

Choke is the constriction at the muzzle end of a shotgun's barrels. Full choke signifies that the barrels are constricted so much that the cartridge pellets will leave the barrels in a tight pattern and kill targets at a considerable distance. On the other

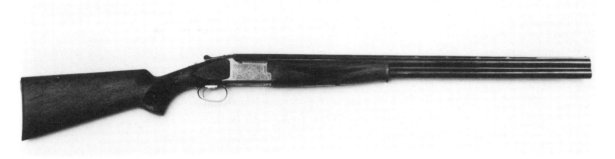

A Sporting shotgun.

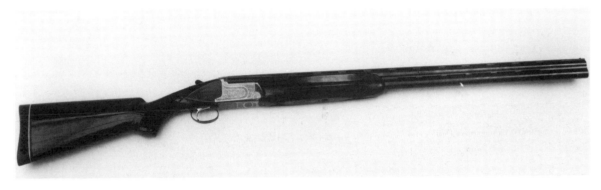

A trap gun.

hand, open choke – or cylinder to give it its correct name – means much less constriction and a shot pattern that spreads quickly as it leaves the barrels, which is ideal for close targets.

In between these two extremes, which have specialist uses in some disciplines – full choke is regarded by many shooters to be essential for the fast receding targets encountered at Olympic Trap – are others, such as quarter and half. This particular combination is favoured by many leading shooters for Sporting clays.

A multichoke gun usually comes with five screw-in chokes: cylinder, quarter, half, three-quarters and full, and the shooter can select the choke combination he requires for the discipline he is shooting.

This clearly has advantages for the beginner who has not decided which discipline he intends to specialize in, if any. If, at a later date, he decides to concentrate on Olympic Trap, he will need a specially designed trap gun with tight, fixed chokes and a stock and rib configuration designed for these particular targets. However, as a first gun, a multichoke enables the novice to experiment in all the disciplines without being particularly disadvantaged.

If you do decide on a multichoke, do not fall into the trap of changing your chokes for every target on a Sporting layout – it is not necessary and there will be enough to think about in the beginning without adding chokes to the list!

You will also need to consider barrel

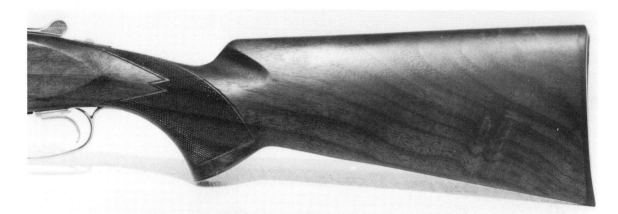

The stock of the Sporter . . .

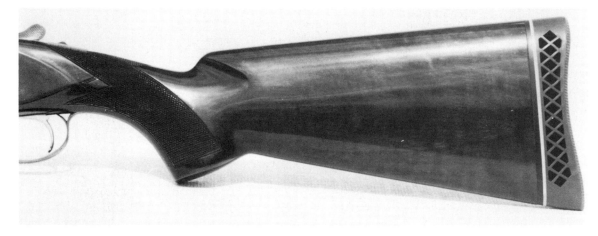

. . . and the trap gun. Note the higher stock.

length. There is a growing trend among top international shooters like A. J. Smith and Mickey Rouse to adopt 32-inch barrels. Remember, though, that they have been shooting for many years and I would suggest you settle on 28 inches for your first gun.

Two other types of shotgun should, in my opinion, be ignored by the novice. The side-by-side, still favoured by many game shooters, is too light for consistent clay shooting and not nearly as pointable as an over-and-under. The side-by-side is rarely seen on clay grounds these days. Semi-automatic shotguns are very effective in the right hands – world championships have been won with them – but they lack the reliability of an over-and-under. The last thing a learner wants is a gun that is prone to malfunction, and semi-autos can leave a lot to be desired in that department.

One other point. Buy the best you can afford. As in everything else, you get what you pay for and an expensive shotgun will handle far better and be much easier to learn with than a cheap one with the

Multichokes can have their advantages — but it is not necessary to change them for every target.

Novices should steer clear of semi-automatics.

handling characteristics of a gatepost. A second-hand gun of superior quality may be a far more sensible buy and do a lot more for your shooting than a cheap new one.

Accessories

Once you have purchased your gun, there are several other accessories you should consider buying before you attend your first shooting event. The first and most important of these is protection for your hearing and it need not cost a fortune. You can spend anything from a few pence for sponge ear-plugs, which are remarkably effective, to more than £100 for electronic ear-muffs which suppress the noise of gunfire but enhance ordinary sounds. In between, there are ear-muffs available for less than £10 and, in scientific tests, these have proved to be more than adequate to protect hearing from the damaging effects of gun-fire.

Many veteran shooters frown upon the use of hearing protectors and are keen to point out that they have never used any form of protection for thirty years or more. The fact that most of them have to lip-read your reply speaks for itself!

Loss of hearing is insidious and cannot be cured. A 12-bore shotgun's peak sound level has been measured at 155 decibels – twenty-five decibels *louder* than Concorde at 100 metres. Because a shotgun report occurs for only a milli-second, its danger is often underestimated. When you consider that you may be firing 100 to 200 cartridges week after week throughout the year, it is patently obvious that protection is vital.

It is the responsibility of shoot organizers . . .

Shooters' eyesight is also at risk from tiny fragments of broken clay, especially on 'driven' stands where incoming targets are broken overhead. Insurance claims for eye injuries have risen steadily in recent years, so reliable shatter-proof shooting glasses are highly desirable. They are available in various tints to enhance target visibility in poor light and against difficult backgrounds, so as well as preventing a nasty injury, they may also increase your scores by making targets more visible.

Finally, there is a noticeable and discouraging trend for competitors to turn up at clay shoots shabbily dressed to say the least. It is an attitude which is detrimental to the image of the sport, so make sure you buy yourself a smart shooting vest made by a company like Ganton. It need not cost the earth and it will do much to enhance the perception of shooting in the public eye. A shooting vest is a sleeveless, comfortable garment with large pockets in which to carry your cartridges. Clay shooting can be enjoyed all the year round, so you may also wish to invest in some lightweight waterproof clothing which keeps out the wind as well as the rain. In my experience, many gunshops do not always carry large stocks of accessories. If you have difficulty obtaining the excellent waterproofs marketed by companies such as Gunmark and Browning, try your local golf shop for a similar product. They will have just the thing. Unfortunately, shooting has many opponents and a clay ground frequented by people who appear at first sight to be nothing more than slovenly layabouts does not help its image. Be proud of yourself and your sport.

Cartridges

Until the beginning of 1988, it was admissible to use 32-gram shot loads for all the clay disciplines. Then the ISU ruled that 28-gram cartridges, commonly known as 1-ounce loads, must be used for Olympic Trap. Twelve months later, the governing bodies of all other disciplines, except FITASC, followed suit. As a result, the 28-gram cartridge is now compulsory for all disciplines apart from FITASC Sporting, where 36-gram loads are permissible and still used by many French FITASC shooters.

One very real advantage of the lighter load is reduced recoil, and many shooters who originally doubted the efficacy of 28-gram cartridges are now more than satisfied with their performance. Proof of their effectiveness is borne out by the fact that scores have not deteriorated in any discipline since their introduction.

When you are choosing a cartridge, select the best you can afford from one of the multitude of well-known brands on the market. You will find it far cheaper to buy in bulk, so try to purchase at least a thousand at a time and split them, and the cost, with a friend. You will make a considerable saving if you buy your cartridges in this way.

. . . to ensure that trappers are adequately protected.

29

SAFETY – YOUR MOST IMPORTANT LESSON

The big day has arrived and you are on the shooting ground with your own gun for the very first time. You will probably be excited and a little apprehensive, and it is now that you must remember the golden rules for safe shooting.

Some people have the mistaken belief that a shotgun will only break clays. It is worth considering, then, that ballistics experts have compared the destructive force of a shotgun cartridge to a grenade. Shotguns are designed for killing and, as such, must be treated with the greatest respect and common sense for your own and other shooters' safety.

Clay shooting has had a remarkably healthy safety record over the years and this is owing to the good sense of competitors and their willingness to adhere to safety rules which apply on all clay-pigeon shooting grounds. Never forget that:

● All guns must be open and empty except when the competitor is on the shooting stand and facing the direction of the target flight-path.
● Over-and-under and side-by-side shotguns must be broken and unloaded at all other times.
● Semi-automatic and pump-action guns must be open at the breech and the muzzle pointed straight up in the air or down at the ground.
● At Sporting events, you must carry your gun from stand to stand in a gun-slip.
● All guns should be treated as if they are loaded and should *never*, in any circumstances, be pointed at another person.

It is sensible to attend your first few events with an experienced shooter who can stand behind you on the shooting stand to prevent you turning away from the target area with a loaded gun. I have seen novices miss a target with their first barrel and then turn around to seek advice – with their second barrel still undischarged. An experienced shot behind you on the stand can prevent this potentially lethal manoeuvre.

Safe gun-handling must become absolutely instinctive. Never underestimate the ability of a shotgun to maim and kill. It is the responsibility of people organizing shoots to do so in the safest possible way. Targets must be safe for shooters and spectators alike wherever they are shot, and trappers must be adequately protected.

This book is not an instructional manual. Its purpose is to give both novice and experienced shooter an indication of the robust health of clay shooting today, as well as an insight into its various disciplines.

In the subsequent chapters of this book, the disciplines are described in more detail by the individual shooters who have excelled at them and who have become champions at either national or international levels. Their knowledge and experience have been accumulated as a result of years of competitive shooting at the highest level. All of them have demonstrated the qualities of outstanding skill and dedication which are required to reach the very top in their respective chosen disciplines. The advice that they dispense should prove to be invaluable at whatever level you choose to compete in the exciting sport of clay pigeon shooting.

1 English Sporting

By George Digweed

George Digweed achieved national recognition towards the end of the 1988 season when he won the World Sporting Jubilee. That victory was followed in 1989 with an incredible 'double' when George won both the British and English Open Sporting Championships with record scores, dropping a total of only seven targets in both 100-bird events. He has also won the EC and UK FITASC Grands Prix and been a member of the England Skeet Team.

English sporting is by far the most popular form of clay shooting in the United Kingdom. It offers an extensive variety of targets and, because it does not require permanent installation of traps or shooting stands, it can be relatively cheap and easy to stage.

In its simplest form, it may be a 20-bird competition on a flat field at a village fête. At its best and most challenging, it could be the British Open Sporting Championship, contested over a series of 100 very difficult targets at one of our premier shooting grounds.

English Sporting is by far the most popular form of clay shooting.

Two stands in action on an English Sporting layout.

George Digweed on a wooded stand in the British Open Sporting Championship.

Both may be described as English Sporting, but you can rest assured that there the similarity ends. There is an enormous gulf between small local re-entry competitions and the major championship events. Because you perform well at your village fête it certainly does not mean that you could do the same at the British Open. The two are light-years apart, and to graduate successfully from one to the other will take much hard work. First you must learn the basics of sound shooting technique – precise gun mounting, correct footwork – and then develop an ability to 'read' targets correctly.

You must be prepared to travel to different grounds, and enter many competitions in order to experience as wide a variety of targets as possible. Travelling to shoot really is an essential part of your learning curve. Many shooters who put in respectable scores at the same ground week after week do so only because they are familiar with the targets – take them to another venue and they are lost.

I am a great believer in Sporting shooters learning another discipline first because there is no doubt that the type of regular shooting required in a discipline teaches competent gun mounting, footwork and most of all concentration. I started shooting skeet as a diversion from Sporting and, in two years, I shot nineteen 100 straights, including one on my first appearance in the England Team. I am certain that shooting in this discipline has contributed to my success at Sporting and it has definitely helped my concentration.

The organizers of Sporting shoots are largely governed by the natural features of their land in deciding the type of targets they are able to put on. Targets should be designed to simulate the flight of birds in the field. One stand may have a pair of

Roundwood, one of Britain's premier Sporting grounds, boasts a 128-foot tower – the highest in the country.

It appears to be a very high pheasant, judging by the shooter's position.

driven grouse and another a going-away bird with a rabbit 'on report', which means that the rabbit is not released from its trap until the report of the gun firing at the first target has been heard. Suddenly switching your gun from the high target to shoot down at a fast, bolting rabbit will certainly test the shooter's gun handling, and you would be surprised how many good shooters are caught out by a bunny! Combinations of targets from opposite directions which have to be killed in different places frequently offer a searching examination of a shooter's footwork.

My favourite shooting grounds are mid Norfolk, Southdown, High Lodge, Hodnet, Roundwood and Apsley, all venues with outstanding natural features which enhance the quality of the birds. To their great credit, these grounds are always able to test the skill of the shooter without resorting to throwing edge-on midis 50 yards out. Instead, they keep shooters on their toes by using a deceptive mixture of speed and angle; and combinations of different targets – minis, midis, battues and rockets – all of which can give different and illusory impressions of speed.

English Sporting can comprise up to 30 per cent FITASC targets and I am delighted when the full quota is used to deceive the shooter.

A major championship shoot is usually 100 targets over ten stands and when I arrive at an event I always walk around and look at the targets first. I study them all,

from the rabbit and the teal to the crossing magpie and the high pheasant. I like to see where the clays are going and where they are coming from, and then I decide in my mind what sort of score I expect to shoot.

I prefer to shoot late in a championship, so that I can see what scores have already been achieved. If I shoot early and miss a target, I lose confidence a little because I start to tell myself that other shooter's will not miss that particular bird. When I shot at the British Open Championship in 1989, Mickey Rouse had already put a 96 on the board. That would have put some people off, but the more pressure I am under the better I like it. I looked at Mickey's score and told myself I needed to shoot a 97 to

Always check out the targets before you shoot them yourself.

A. J. Smith makes sure he knows where the bird is coming from.

win – and I did. The pressure makes me shoot better because it helps me to concentrate; and the bigger the crowd watching me, the more I enjoy it. Their very presence makes me more determined not to make a hash of things!

I really do think it is very important to walk round and check the targets before shooting. On some stands, it is vitally important to pick up a target as soon as possible and it assists your preparation to watch other people shooting first. You are not suddenly surprised, then, by the target that needs shooting very early, which just might have got away if you had not bothered to check it out beforehand. It also helps you to decide how you are going to shoot each stand. I shoot different targets with a different method and always try to

I prefer to shoot late, to see what scores have been achieved.

35

Gives one a thirst, Sporting shooting. George Digweed and A. J. Smith refresh themselves between stands.

Winning is always pleasant – George Digweed receiving a prize from Gunmark's Brian Hebditch.

kill the target in the easiest place. On some stands, that may mean shooting the target very fast. On others, I may decide to allow the bird to come to the end of its flight before I kill it. Wherever I think is the best place to kill it, I am prepared.

Some novice shooters miss birds because they have a tendency to mount their guns before they have seen the target. It is absolutely essential that they pick up the bird with their eyes, not the flight line it is taking – whether it is dipping in the wind, for instance – and then mount and squeeze the trigger as they swing through it. The novice is making things very difficult for himself if he insists on mounting his gun before he has seen the target and that is another reason why I suggest that a young person should learn to shoot a discipline before attempting to succeed at Sporting.

Because the flight of the targets does not vary, skeet will teach the novice to prepare correctly for every bird, to become consistent with his gun mounting and also to swing smoothly as he mounts. If the novice masters these basics first on a skeet layout, he will be far better prepared for the variety of English Sporting targets, and he will certainly start to record higher scores much sooner.

Many shooters also underestimate the necessity of having a reasonable standard of physical fitness. Shooting requires mental fitness and that, in turn, requires physical well-being so look after yourself and exercise regularly. I follow quite a strict keep-fit regime which involves playing a lot of squash and I am sure it has helped to prepare me for shooting. It is no use suggesting that this would work for everybody, but to keep reasonably fit makes sense anyway.

Once your scores do become more consistent, get the feel for competition by

George Digweed preparing to shoot off in the British Open Sporting Championships with Gary Phillips. Gary won.

Barry Simpson, an English Sporting ace before switching to FITASC.

shooting in registered events. If you are a member of the Clay Pigeon Shooting Association – and if you are shooting clays regularly you certainly should be – you will be classified according to your score in these events. If you score under 60 per cent, you will be in Class C; score 60–67 per cent and you will be in Class B; higher than that and under 75 per cent and you will be in Class A. To reach Class AA in English Sporting, you need to score 75 per cent and over, which is a consistently high standard of shooting.

It says a lot for the quality of English Sporting shooters that many, like Barry Simpson, A. J. Smith, and Mickey Rouse, have gone on to win the FITASC Sporting World Championship. I believe they have become outstanding performers at the international version of Sporting because of the lessons they learned shooting English Sporting, which is a purely domestic discipline.

Although I shoot FITASC Sporting myself, and have won some major competitions, I still prefer the home-grown version. It has one great advantage over other forms of clay shooting: wherever you live in the United Kingdom, you will certainly be able to find a Sporting shoot being staged within a reasonable distance most Sunday mornings.

2 FITASC Sporting

By Mickey Rouse

Mickey Rouse has excelled at every clay discipline he has chosen to shoot. However, in 1990 he surpassed even his own illustrious performances by completing the FITASC 'Grand Slam.' He won both the World and European FITASC Sporting Championships and the World Cup in one amazing season. He has won the English Skeet and British Open Sporting Championships and, in 1989, another memorable 'double' year, he was both English and British FITASC Sporting Champion.

A certain mystique has grown up around FITASC Sporting, which serves either to frighten people off or to encourage them to compete. Unfortunately, many English Sporting shooters who are persuaded to enter a FITASC competition expect to record high scores immediately. When that does not happen, they are often so dispirited by their comparatively poor performance that they are put off the discipline for good. Take it from me: you are in for a big surprise if you expect to move straight from English Sporting to FITASC and start putting in comparable scores. FITASC is a completely different form of competition, a discipline where no two targets are the same and where your all-round shooting skill will be tested to its limit.

There is certainly no doubt that English Sporting is an indispensable and invaluable preparation. It will teach you the fundamental rules for tackling the wide variety of targets you can expect in FITASC. But if you are to shoot FITASC seriously you must be prepared to start learning all over again.

In FITASC you will encounter targets, angles and combinations that will not only test your gun handling, your footwork and your ability to shoot fluently, but also your aptitude for 'reading' birds. It is the *crème de la crème* of Sporting shooting. Not only is every target different, but so is its speed, angle and trajectory.

Because it is so challenging, I believe a person taking up FITASC must be prepared to persevere for two or three years before he can expect to become really competent. Unfortunately, it is very expensive to shoot regularly and some shooters, who feel they are not getting to grips with it as quickly as they would like, tend to become disheartened and give up. If they can afford it, I would urge them to keep trying and not expect too much for a couple of years at least, and probably longer.

If they do persevere, and eventually find their scores creeping up as they learn to cope with all the FITASC variables, they will never regret it. It is without a doubt the most satisfying and stimulating form of Sporting clay shooting.

FITASC is an abbreviation of the title of the ruling body of international Sporting,

Checking the flight-line of a target, Belgian FITASC shooter Thierry de Latre and Britain's Tina Merrick.

the Federation de Tir aux Armes Sportives de Chasse, a Paris-based organization which is also responsible for the trap discipline of Universal Trench.

There has been an amazing growth in the popularity of FITASC all over the world in recent years, and when I won the World Championship at Le Rabot in France in 1990 there was a record entry of more than 720 shooters from Great Britain, France, Austria, Switzerland, Cyprus, Holland, the USA, Australia and New Zealand.

Ironically, this tremendous interest and the increasingly large number of people who now wish to shoot competitions have given FITASC a very real problem. So much so that they have had to devise a

Scores will drop when you start shooting FITASC.

39

With his gun down, a shooter prepares for the singles on a FITASC stand.

'new' system for the organization and running of shoots in order to accommodate more and more competitors.

Established FITASC shooters, regular competitors on the European circuit, were not happy when the new system was first introduced. And although I am one who still prefers to shoot what is known as the 'old' system, I really believe that FITASC's administrators had little alternative but to devise another method of staging competitions in the face of the growing number of people wishing to shoot the discipline. If the targets remain as challenging as those traditionally associated with FITASC, then I do not think the system can be faulted.

After a false start when it was first introduced, and a consequent loss of target variety, the birds were definitely back to their best under the new system in the World and European Championships in France and Cyprus in 1990.

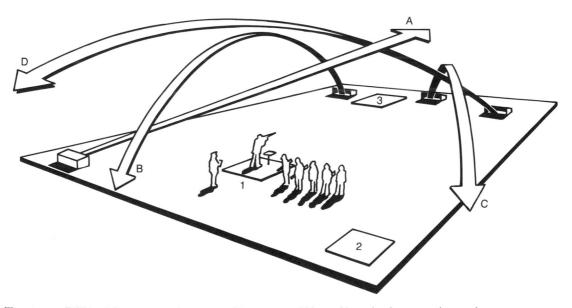

Targets on a FITASC layout. In reality, none of the traps would be visible to the shooter, and natural features of the land would be used to enhance the targets. This example has been drawn flat for simplicity. Note how the targets vary as the shooters move from stand to stand. For instance, the going-away target from trap A on stand 1 becomes a 'driven' bird on stand 3, while the oncoming targets from traps B, C and D become going-away birds of one kind or another.

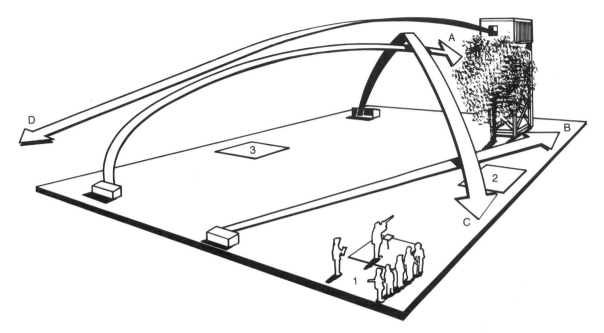

A typical round of twenty-five FITASC targets on this layout could comprise:

Stand 1: singles: C, normal; B, rabbit; D, midi; A, battue.
  Doubles: C, normal; B, rabbit; D, midi; A, battue.

Stand 2: singles: A, battue; B, rabbit; C, midi; D, normal.
  Doubles: B, rabbit; C, midi; D, normal; C, midi.

Stand 3: singles: A, battue; B, rabbit; C, normal; D, normal; C, midi
  Doubles: D, normal; B, rabbit; C, midi; B, rabbit.

It may be helpful if I describe both systems, because many shooting grounds in the UK still adhere to the original method of staging FITASC.

First, the old system: a 25-bird layout will consist of three shooting stands and four or five traps. The angle and direction of targets will alter as shooters move from one stand to another.

The squad of six competitors will shoot in strict rotation on each stand, starting with single targets on stand one, in the following order: 1, 2, 3, 4, 5, 6. When the squad move on to stand 2, the singles there are shot first by competitor No. 3, and so on. There are usually four singles and two doubles on each stand, although an extra single may be shot on one stand to bring

the total for the layout to twenty-five targets.

Only one squad is allowed on a layout at a time and, consequently, two shooting stands remain vacant while a squad is shooting the third. There are four layouts for a 100-bird competition and the numbered squads shoot each at a pre-determined time.

The new system has been described by its critics as nothing more than squadded English Sporting. Each stand on a particular layout is totally separate, with its own targets and its own traps, just as in English Sporting. As soon as one squad has shot and moved on to another stand, another six shooters immediately take their place. In this way, every stand is permanently

Another trophy: Mickey Rouse receives his cup for winning the 1989 Browning Masters competition.

occupied, and more shooters can be accommodated.

This system requires a lot of space to be staged satisfactorily; otherwise shoot organizers cannot offer the variety of targets one associates with FITASC. As far as I am concerned the French and Cypriots have proved that target quality can be maintained and the French achievement in putting 120 squads through eight layouts in less than three days in the 1990 World Championships was unbelievable.

So what can you expect when you walk on to a shooting stand in a FITASC competition for the first time? If you happen to be the first shooter on your squad, the referee will show you the four singles you are about to shoot.

You will call for your targets in the usual way, and it is here that you will encounter the biggest physical difference between FITASC and English Sporting: the targets must be called for gun down. In other words, the stock must be out of your shoulder and touching your body below the armpit. What is more, it is against the rules to move before you see the target, so do not mount in anticipation if you hear the trap but cannot see the bird.

Remember that you do have full use of

the gun on the singles, so do not hesitate to second barrel a target if you miss with your first shot. Having shot the singles first, you will be the last shooter on the squad to shoot the doubles, which can be an advantage because it will give you the opportunity to watch where other shooters kill the targets.

You will probably feel quite tense on your first FITASC layout. Do not worry about it. As you shoot the discipline more, and become familiar with the variety of targets, you will start to relax and enjoy it. I am not saying that you will find it easy. It took me two full seasons even to get into

the top ten at FITASC. Then, after winning the British Open Sporting in 1988, I decided that I wanted a Great Britain badge and the only way I could win one at Sporting was to get into the FITASC team.

Since 1988, I have shot with 32-inch barrels choked three-quarters and full, which is very tight for Sporting shooting, but which I feel is just right for some of the very hard FITASC targets. For many years, I shot with a 29-inch gun and watched top Sporting shooters like Gary Phillips and Carl Bloxham using 32-inch barrels to kill targets I could not hit.

I ordered some 32-inch barrels myself

The referee shows the targets to the first shooter – in this case Brian Hebditch – on a FITASC squad.

Gary Phillips, wizard with a 32-inch gun, won the British Open in 1990.

intending to have them bored out to a quarter and half and I used them for the first time when I won the English FITASC Championship at John Bidwell's High Lodge Shooting Ground. I finished six targets in front of A. J. Smith, who was World Champion for the second time that season, and decided to leave the barrels as they were!

For many years I have shot skeet and I believe that it has been a great help to me with my Sporting. If you can get comparatively close and easy targets sorted out, it can obviously be of tremendous benefit to you.

In skeet there are twenty-four different targets and I used to practise by shooting a round straight, then standing back five yards and shooting it straight again. If you are keen enough and willing to work at it like that, you will learn every time you squeeze the trigger. Although I still enjoy shooting skeet and English Sporting, I do not get the same buzz from either discipline anymore.

The trouble with English Sporting for me, and many other FITASC shooters, is the repetition. On a stand where there are five pairs, I can hit the first two or three pairs but then I get bored and start missing. A. J. Smith has exactly the same problem. However, it is our grounding in English Sporting which has made British shooters such outstanding performers at FITASC. We really are the best in the world, and one glance at the juniors who are already coming through convinces me that we will stay that way for many years to come.

3 Down the Line

By Dick Fletton

Dick Fletton, who now shoots Universal Trench and Olympic Trap, was an outstanding Down-the-Line shooter. He won the English DTL Championship in 1988 and was runner-up on three occasions. He won the British Single-Barrel Championship twice, in 1984 and 1985, and also the English and British Double-Rise Championships.

Because the targets are relatively straight-forward, Down the Line (DTL) tends to be the starting point for all the other clay shooting disciplines. It helps a shooter to develop a sound basic technique, teaches him to mount his gun correctly and is invaluable in perfecting a smooth swing.

More than anything else, however, it teaches concentration and mental discipline. In DTL, a first-barrel kill scores three points and a second barrel, two points. In top-level competition, a score of 100/300, that is one hundred first-barrel kills, is commonplace. So not only must you kill

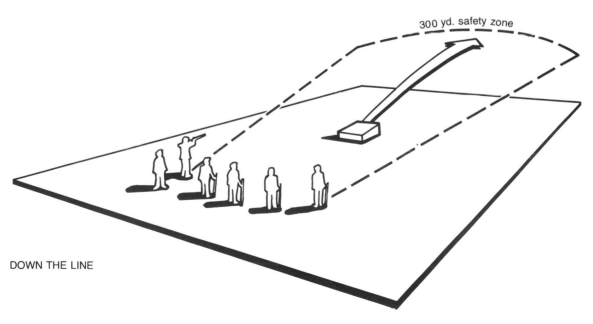

DOWN THE LINE

A typical DTL layout.

every target to have a hope of succeeding, you must kill them all with your first barrel! Believe me, that standard of shooting on a regular basis takes the most intense concentration.

All the basics you learn at DTL will stand you in good stead no matter what discipline you shoot in the future. Every competitor, whether shooting Olympic Trap or FITASC Sporting, will benefit from the fundamental lessons of DTL.

The targets are thrown from a single trap 16 yards in front of a squad of five shooters. They are not fast and, judged by the standards of other trap disciplines, the angles at which the targets emerge from the trap are not too taxing. A normal round of DTL is twenty-five targets, with each competitor shooting five targets from each of five shooting stands.

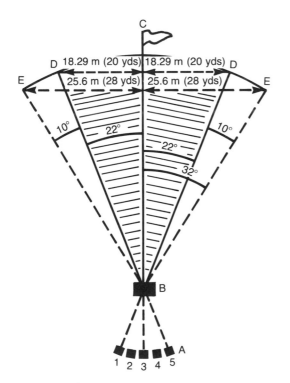

Dimensions for DTL.

One of the reasons that DTL is such a valuable learning discipline is that it requires regular, unhurried shooting for success. Stance, gun mount and swing must become second nature. If all these requirements are fulfilled, a shooter should soon start to record quite high scores. But where 21 or 22 out of 25 may be quite respectable at, say, English Sporting, it is just not good enough at DTL. That is where the concentration comes in, especially in a competition over 100 targets. To stand even a chance of success, every target must be killed, and preferably, of course, with the first barrel.

Everything must be perfectly right in your mind before you call for your bird otherwise you are risking a dropped target or a lost point, either of which could be disastrous in competition.

I started shooting DTL by entering 10-bird re-entry shoots and I became absorbed by it. Then I did what anyone who wishes to shoot the discipline seriously should do: I bought a trap gun, a Browning with 32-inch barrels. My first time out with it was a 100-bird competition at Nottingham and I shot a 100/299. Those small events had clearly helped to develop my powers of concentration.

When I am shooting DTL I do the same thing for every single target. I stand with the weight on my forward foot so that I feel comfortable (if you feel comfortable, your stance should be just about right). Then I set myself up for the worst target possible on the particular peg I am shooting. For instance, on peg 1, a right-hand bird out of the trap is a straight target from my shooting position. In this case, I prepare myself for the target which will be thrown to the left out of the trap, so that I can swing my gun on to it easily. The correct preparation for every target on every peg is absolutely essential.

I always mount my gun 2 or 3 feet above

Everything must be just right in your mind before you call for the bird.

the trap-house. On peg 1, I would mount on the top left-hand corner of it, so if a target did come off the trap and fly to the left I would be in a comfortable position to deal with it. Similarly, on peg 5, the difficult bird would be a right-hander, so I would point the gun above the top right-hand corner of the trap-house, ready to swing straight on to the target going right.

As you shoot DTL, you will soon come to know which are the difficult target angles on particular pegs and learn to prepare yourself for them. This preparation, together with accurate gun mounting and a fluent swing, is part of the total concentration necessary for each target.

Once you have shot DTL regularly and decided that you want to shoot it seriously, I think you should go to a competent coach. Some people have a natural ability to shoot, and learning will come easily to them. Those who do not have inherent talent, but make up for it with great enthusiasm for the sport, will have to work harder for their knowledge and expertise. Such people will find a good coach of tremendous assistance.

I would always recommend trap shooting to a novice, because there are so many different disciplines for a shooter to progress to when he feels the time has come to move on to something new. If you decide to concentrate for a time on DTL, your

Keep your eye on the target at all times.

ultimate goal must be to represent your country; one of the highest honours I achieved at DTL was being high gun of the England Team in 1985. You may progress to Automatic Ball Trap (ABT), and have the thrill and excitement of learning something different but for which DTL has prepared you well. Again your goal may be the England team.

Then you can move on to the international disciplines like Universal Trench and Olympic Trap. Here, there is the possibility of shooting for Great Britain and the opportunity to shoot against the finest performers in the world. You may be fortunate enough to compete against a world champion – a fantastic experience.

In trap shooting, there is always a new mountain to climb; you have never finished. I know Sporting is the most popular discipline, but it cannot offer the on-going challenge that trap shooting does. Sporting shooters can move on to FITASC Sporting, but that is their lot. In trap there is always something new to be

Set yourself up for the most difficult target on a particular peg.

DTL is an outstanding teacher.

In trap shooting, there is always a new mountain to climb.

tackled, something fresh to be learned and, at the end of the road, there are the Olympic and Commonwealth games.

While on the subject of Sporting, it is interesting to note that most Sporting shooters have difficulty with going-away targets. I am quite sure many of them would benefit from DTL shooting. As I said earlier, it really is the starting point for all clay shooting, an outstanding teacher whatever your chosen discipline.

Because they involve the use of only one trap and are therefore relatively inexpensive to set up, there are excellent DTL layouts at shooting grounds all over the British Isles so the novice should not have any difficulty finding somewhere to shoot.

If you are going to shoot the discipline regularly, it is essential that you have the right tools for the job so get yourself a trap gun. Make sure that the choking is not too tight – half and three-quarters is adequate for DTL targets – and I would recommend 32-inch barrels. They are probably a little too slow for the faster trap disciplines like

Universal Trench and Olympic Trap, but are just right for DTL, giving the nice steady swing necessary for the slower, less angled going-away targets.

When you are actually shooting, concentrate on the job in hand. Do not count your shots and do not keep score. Your purpose is to kill the next target, so prepare for it carefully and tell yourself that you are going to kill it. When you are not shooting, watch people who are obviously good to see how they do it. You may be able to adapt some of their techniques to suit you, but do not expect everything they do to be exactly right for you.

At first, I tried mounting my gun like Keith Bond, who is a brilliant DTL shot, with the muzzles pointed right at the top of the trap-house, but it was never successful for me and targets were getting away.

The cage and wooden posts prevent the shooter bringing his gun back into a dangerous position.

I experimented and eventually adopted a much higher gun mount, 2 or 3 feet above the trap-house. That was far more suitable for me and I have continued to mount like that throughout my shooting career. So do not be disappointed if you see an experienced shot doing something which is clearly right for him but is a disaster for you. A slight adaptation can make all the difference, and again this is where a competent coach can be invaluable.

Whatever you do, make sure you relax when you are shooting. If you are tense your gun mounting and swing will be inhibited. It is only a sport, after all. So be relaxed as you bring the gun up and, when you call 'Pull', and see the target, swing your gun smoothly by moving your body from the waist and not by raising your arms. As your muzzles blot out the target, pull the trigger and kill it. Then start concentrating immediately on the most important bird of all – the next one. You will soon be on your way to your first 100/300!

4 Olympic Trap

By Ian Peel

Ian Peel has consistently proved himself one of our finest Olympic Trap shooters. In the 1986 Commonwealth games in Edinburgh, he won gold medals in the individual and pairs events and, four years later in Auckland, New Zealand, he won Commonwealth gold in the pairs and bronze in the individual competition. He also shot for Great Britain in the 1988 Olympic games in Seoul. He has won the British Olympic Trap Grand Prix and is a top-flight performer at Automatic Ball Trap. He won the British ABT Championship in 1986 with 200 straight.

I regard Olympic Trap (OT) as the finest of all the clay shooting disciplines. It is the cream, one of only two disciplines you can shoot in the Olympic and Commonwealth games and in the World and European championships. It also enables you to shoot for your country.

For sheer variety of targets, for speed, for angles and for the intensity of competition I do not think any other discipline touches it. I have shot Trench at the highest level all over the world and can honestly say that I would not have missed a moment of it – and that includes the bitter disappointments, like finishing twenty-fifth in the Olympic games in Seoul, South Korea, because I had peaked several months too soon!

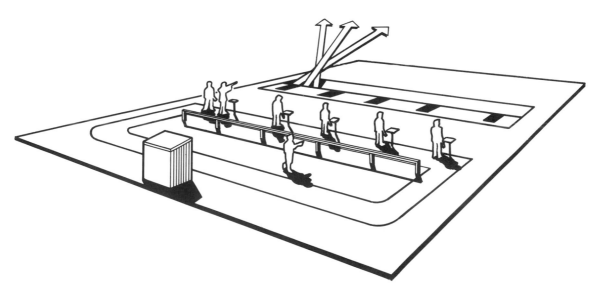

A typical Olympic Trap layout.

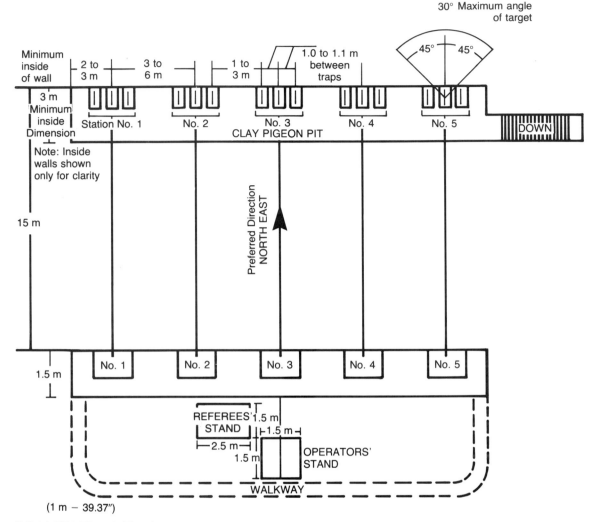

Official ISU Olympic Trap layout.

If you aspire to top-level competition and have the talent and will to succeed, I would urge you to try shooting Olympic Trap. However, but do not make the mistake of thinking you will be able to walk straight on to a layout and start achieving high scores. There is an awful lot of hard work to be done before that happens.

The proven route for a successful Olympic Trap shooter is to graduate through the trap disciplines, starting with DTL, on to ABT, then Universal Trench and so on. In each case, you will be shooting at going-away targets which will increase in speed and angle as you progress.

Most people start shooting with a Sporting gun and use it to try all types of clay shooting. However, once you have decided that you wish to concentrate on trap, you must buy a trap gun specifically designed for trap targets. Then start shooting DTL seriously. It is an outstanding discipline for teaching you concentration. As Dick Fletton says in an earlier chapter, you have to kill every single target with your first barrel to be successful at the highest level, something that takes tremendous application.

I shot DTL for two years and although I was AA Class, which requires an average success rate of 95 per cent and over, I was never good enough to win a place in the England Team, and now that more people are shooting the discipline competition is even tighter at the top.

DTL is the only trap discipline where a first-barrel kill scores higher than a second. In all the others, a second-barrel kill scores exactly the same as a target killed with the first. Believe me, you will have many occasions to be thankful for your second barrel as you watch a particularly fierce OT target receding into the distance despite your first shot!

Once you have learned to shoot trap targets, you will encounter the problem faced by the majority of OT shooters in Great Britain – where to shoot? There are only a handful of OT layouts in the UK so you will be very fortunate indeed if you happen to live near one. Layouts have acoustically released targets and fifteen traps, three for each shooting position, and are consequently very expensive to install. I live in Lancashire and I have to drive more than 100 miles to Beverley in East Yorkshire or ninety miles to the North Wales SS at Sealand, near Chester, in order to practise. There are also grounds with OT layouts at Garlands shooting ground in the Midlands, at Haverfordwest in South Wales and at the Loch Ness Gun Club for those who live north of the border.

As in clay shooting generally, more

It takes seven years to learn to shoot trench properly.

There is no excuse for sloppy mounting.

people than ever are shooting Olympic Trap, something which has been especially noticeable over the last three years. Perhaps this growth in popularity will eventually lead to the opening of more layouts. Let us hope so.

In the meantime, your commitment to the discipline is going to be severely tested by the amount of travelling you have to do for practice and competition. If you have the commitment and are willing to travel and clearly intend to shoot OT seriously, I would suggest that you seek out a good coach and have lessons.

It has been estimated that it takes seven years to learn to shoot Trench properly. It took me about five years without lessons, but I think a good coach can bring a talented DTL shooter along in eighteen months to three years. He will pick up your major faults immediately and also explain why you are missing targets, which is not always obvious to you. There are some excellent coaches in this country like Joe Neville, Peter Boden or Peter Croft and having lessons with a coach of their calibre could accelerate your learning quite considerably.

There are several ways you can help yourself to get the basics right. As in any clay discipline, your gun mount and swing are vitally important and as you pre-mount for OT, this movement especially should be spot-on every time. Dry mounting at home with an unloaded gun can be very beneficial. Bring the gun into your shoulder exactly as you would for a real target, call 'Pull' and swing onto the imaginary bird. This exercise has been recommended for years to assist shooters in all disciplines with their mounting, but now the leading OT nations in the world suggest that shooters should practise in this way for at least half an hour a day and shoot competitions on the other two days!

I also believe that there is a lot to be said for supervised dry shooting of other people's targets on a shooting ground. By

One of the trap layouts at Garlands SG in the Midlands.

Another Garland trap layout.

supervised I mean pre-arranged and under the direction of a coach. Dry shooting someone else's targets can help your timing, especially if you are mounting behind a good shot who is on song. You will hear him call for his bird and see when he shoots it; and you will know if your timing is out if he has shot and killed the target a little earlier or later than when you pulled your trigger on the same bird. This type of dry shooting gives you more targets to shoot at without actually firing your gun so you experience less fatigue from recoil. I cannot stress enough, however, that this exercise *must* be supervised and pre-arranged. Otherwise, never mount your gun on another shooter's target.

What barrel length is best for OT? I firmly believe that 30-inch barrels are ideally suited to the discipline. They have that extra bit of pointability and they have mobility as well, which means you are able to swing fast on to a target. A 30-inch gun is not too heavy and does not get affected by the wind as much as a 32-inch. I do not really understand why some shooters favour a 32-inch gun for OT because I believe that such long barrels have inherent drawbacks. They slow down the swing and tend to control the shooter rather than vice versa.

The best trap shooters in the world are the Italians. There arc something like 1.5 million clay shooters in Italy using some of

Kevin Gill, a Commonwealth Games gold medallist with Ian Peel.

the finest layouts in the world and, because there are so many people shooting, the level of achievement gets pushed higher and higher all the time. The Italians must have twenty world-class OT shooters, and I have never seen an Italian with a 32-inch gun.

I would suggest chokes of three-quarters and full (you will need more choke for OT targets than for DTL) and recommend No. 7 cartridges. It is very important that you do not economize on your cartridges and always use the best you can afford. There are some excellent ones on the market so find one that suits you and stick with it. You will soon come to know what you can expect of the cartridge you feel happiest with.

Trap shooting, especially at competition level, can be a gruelling experience. Sometimes you have to shoot 200 targets in two days, 100 each day. The stress of the competition itself, combined with the concentration and general stamina required to shoot four layouts in a day, can be surprisingly tiring. In OT, shooters are actually pre-mounting their guns into their faces; the recoil is absorbed by the face and shoulders and can cause sustained discomfort.

Since the beginning of 1989, OT shooters have been restricted to the use of 28-gram cartridges, which are generally compulsory throughout clay shooting now, apart from FITASC Sporting. The use of the lighter load has gone a long way towards reducing the fatigue experienced during a shoot. When the new 28-gram loads were introduced, there was a widespread belief that they would lead to a deterioration in scores, especially in the world of fast, receding trap targets. I was as apprehensive as anyone, but any doubts I had about the killing power of the ounce loads were dispelled as soon as I started using them. I shot 198 out of 200 at a selection shoot at Haverfordwest, a total which bettered my highest-ever score with traditional 32-gram cartridges. When you consider that no one has ever achieved a 199 at OT with any size of load in this country it tends to put the whole issue into perspective.

Perhaps some of the second-barrel kills are not quite as spectacular as they were with the heavier load – targets are breaking instead of disappearing in a puff of dust – but the benefits to the shooter, less fatigue and increased accuracy with the second shot, far outweigh the supposed disadvantages of the lighter load.

There is another positive and very important aspect of the smaller cartridges. A No. 7 trap cartridge contains 383 pellets in the 32-gram load compared with 340 in the ounce, so there are considerable environmental advantages in that the lighter load causes considerably less lead pollution. I do not think the scores in any discipline have suffered since the introduction of the 28-gram cartridge, and even a lot of FITASC shooters are using them even though it is not compulsory for that discipline.

Even though there is less physical wear and tear during a long competition, it is vitally important to keep as fit as possible. There is no doubt that if you are physically fit you will find it much easier to cope mentally with the strain of top-level shooting.

Swimming, running and gymnasium work are all beneficial but it is important that you do the correct type of exercise at the gym. Bicycle work is helpful in building up stamina and you will also benefit from small-weight training – it is surprising how tiring lifting an eight-pound gun 100 times a day can be. Keeping a reasonable fitness level definitely helps to sharpen the mind and can make all the difference between success and failure.

As I said earlier, consistent Olympic Trap shooting starts with precise gun mounting. Remember, the rules state that you have fifteen seconds to mount and if you do not get it exactly right the first time, you can lower the gun and mount again. In other words, there is absolutely no excuse for sloppy mounting.

One other golden rule: never chase an OT target out of the trap. It is a certain way to miss behind because you will only be moving at the same speed as the target. Instead, let the clay go for about 10 yards and then swing through it. The very fact that you start from behind means that you will swing faster than the target is moving in order to catch it. Pull the trigger as your muzzles reach it and you should kill it.

5 Universal Trench

By John Grice

John Grice became the first Briton to win the UT World Championship on Italian soil at Lonato in 1990, an achievement graphically described by one magazine as shooting's equivalent of climbing Mount Everest without oxygen and wearing plimsolls! He has won the British Championship three times and the English twice. He had previously shot Down the Line and Automatic Ball Trap for England and first qualified for the British Universal Trench Team in 1981. He also shoots Olympic Trap.

Wherever trap shooters gather, there will always be a discussion about which is the harder discipline, Universal Trench or Olympic Trap. It is a question which stimulates lively debate but since both disciplines are very testing and require extraordinary concentration and fast, precise shooting at each and every target, I do not really think there is much to separate them. Having said that, I do feel it is marginally harder to shoot UT because targets emerge from the traps at far more acute angles.

There are five traps at UT, instead of the fifteen in Olympic Trap, but where an OT bird is thrown off one of three traps directly in front of the shooter, a UT target can come off any one of the five. Consequently, the birds are thrown in a far wider arc. Once you see a target, the chances are that you will have to swing your gun much further than in OT in order to catch and kill it.

In many ways, of course, UT is very similar to OT. It is shot in the same way, with competitors moving to their right after each shot and then from peg 5 behind the firing line to peg 1. But because the targets are likely to cross the centre-point

you have a much wider area to watch for your bird. I call it the killing area and I look out at it in a soft focus as I call for the target. In that way, I see the whole arc in which the target will fly and also see the bird the moment it emerges from the trap, whichever way it is going.

The way you set yourself up for each shot is vitally important. You must see the whole of the killing zone, so do not look down the rib of your gun. Look out in front of you, over your barrels, so you will be on to the target visually the split second it appears. I mount my gun on the lip of the trap-house and look out 3 or 4 feet above that. In other words, I am looking through the gun for the target to appear and when it does I tend to shoot it very quickly indeed.

Having said that, you must never fall into the trap of moving your gun *before* you see the target. You could be the fastest shot in the world by anticipating the bird but it will count for nothing if you are not killing it. If you do anticipate the target, the chances are you will be swinging in the wrong direction when it does leave the trap. And never try to 'read' the targets. Because the shooter to your left has just had a left-hander, it does not necessarily mean you will get a right-hander. Always see the target before moving your gun. My motto is very simple but effective: see it, kill it.

Before you think of shooting a discipline as testing as Trench, it is essential that you have your gun fitted so that it becomes almost an extension of your body. In Italy, many of the top trap shooters go to the Perazzi factory and have themselves measured and their guns custom fitted. Obviously we are not able to do that, but I would advise anyone buying a gun not to go to a High Street shop and expect to be fitted exactly to their requirements. Instead, I would suggest that you visit a shooting ground like Garlands SG near Tamworth, Staffordshire, where there is a shop and trap shooters behind the counter to advise and help you make your choice. Because they shoot themselves, they know what a shooter needs and can give you invaluable help in making your choice.

The chances are that a ground like Garlands will also have a coach in attendance who will be able to give you helpful basic advice and start you off with sound technique. Start first on the slower trap disciplines like DTL and ABT before attempting UT because leading trap shooters like Ian Peel, Dick Fletton and my great shooting partner Kevin Borley came up that way. Disciplines like that teach you to concentrate and to persevere. I shot nineteen 99s before I got my first 100 straight at DTL and followed that with twenty-eight 100s before moving up to UT.

As you progress, it is also very important to get your mental attitude right. before I shoot, I sit and relax with my eyes closed and visualize each clay coming off the trap. In my mind, I am killing them as I see them. When you walk on to the layout you must do so with total belief in

John Grice – 'I think UT is marginally harder than OT'.

yourself. You must prepare to shoot, thinking: I can kill anything that comes.

If there is a particularly hard target on a layout you must not go to shoot worrying about it. Before I start shooting, I kill the hard target in my mind and it relaxes me so that when I do go on to the layout I have psyched myself into believing I can shoot everything. Go out without confidence and you are beaten before you start, so take a little time before the shoot to prepare yourself mentally. If you do drop a target, do not let it get out of proportion. Just keep calm, do not start rushing, and keep shooting as smoothly and consistently as possible.

When I won my World Championship in Italy, the pressure was tremendous on the final layout because I knew that if I shot 25 straight the Italians had to do the same to equal my score and force a shoot-off. On my first layout I had shot a 24 – I missed the seventeenth target out – but was determined not to allow that miss to get to me. Before I started the last twenty-five targets I closed my eyes and shot them all in my mind – including the one that had got away earlier!

It takes practice to be able to relax like that at such a vital stage of a world championship but I believe it helped me to tackle that final layout with renewed vigour and confidence. There is certainly much to be said for persevering with relaxation techniques even if they do not appear to be working for you at first.

Shooting at the top can mean a lot of pressure and stress and in 1984 I reached a stage where I was not actually enjoying my shooting any more. It was becoming an ordeal to me. Sport should be enjoyable or there is absolutely no point in carrying on, so I decided to take a break from competitive trap shooting to try to rekindle my enthusiasm for it. For a year I relaxed and shot a little bit of skeet and Sporting, purely for my own pleasure. Then I realized that my heart was still in trap shooting and that I was missing major competitions. The break had made me hungry again. It did me immeasurable good and now I enjoy my shooting more than ever. I am more able to take things in my stride and keep the disappointments in proportion.

I suppose the biggest change the sport has seen in the last few years has been the introduction of 28-gram cartridge loads. They have brought about a tremendous reduction in recoil, especially for trap

When you walk on to a layout, you must have total belief in yourself.

Kevin Borley moved up from DTL and ABT.

shooters who always pre-mount their guns before calling for a target, and the kills are excellent. Lighter loads also cause less muzzle flip from the first shot so you can re-align on the target much quicker for a second. I know it only takes a fraction of a second, but the ability to get on to the bird quickly with your second barrel can make the difference between a kill or a miss.

I suppose there will always be a debate as to what type of shot is required for trap targets, lead or nickel. It all comes down to personal preference, although I always use nickel shot in both barrels to make sure I am able to break the extra hard clays that you will often find abroad. My advice is to stick with a good-quality cartridge and not to keep changing brand. Once you have confidence in them, stick with them.

Shooting can be made quite difficult in bad light, whether the sun is too bright or the day is dull. Most shooting grounds have a varying contrast of colours in front of the shooting layouts and this is where shooting in coloured glasses may be an advantage to you. Tinted lenses can enable you to see the target more clearly against these backgrounds. In Italy, for instance, there were five layouts with a green background, but on three others the background was a sandbank and the targets could not be seen very clearly. I mainly use target orange lenses. Other people favour vermilion or yellow when the light is very bad. Again, it is a matter of deciding what suits you the best and sticking to it.

Despite all my success, I do still have a bogey bird. If there is a trap target I am liable to miss, it is the straight, going-away bird. I think it is the hardest target in any trap shooter's 25 because it is edge on as it leaves the trap. Because of the speed at which I shoot, I have a tendency to flick my barrel and shoot over the top of it. Luckily, it does not happen very often, and it has *never* happened when I am shooting those twenty-five imaginary birds to relax myself before a competition!

6 English and ISU Skeet

By Joe Neville

Joe Neville started shooting as a young boy on his family's farm. Since 1989, he has been national coach for Great Britain's Olympic Trap and ISU Skeet shooting teams. He is admirably qualified for the position having been a member of ISU Skeet teams for three Olympics and a gold, silver and bronze medallist in three Commonwealth Games. He has his own shooting school in the Derbyshire Peak District and was the first person to shoot 200 straight under current ISU Skeet regulations.

Skeet is an excellent discipline for teaching a young shooter good footwork, balance and hand-and-eye co-ordination, which are all qualities essential to competent shooting of any kind.

The ISU Skeet 'ready' position, demonstrated by Joe Neville.

Before attempting ISU Skeet, the novice shooter should become proficient at shooting English Skeet where the targets are much slower than in the international version. An ISU target moves twice as fast as an English Skeet target over the first 20 metres, which is roughly the area where the shooter should kill it. It is obviously far easier to learn to shoot correctly on a slower target than on a fast one, because if you set out to shoot a bird which is too fast for you, it will have a detrimental effect on your gun mounting. I always tell people that in English Skeet you have time to make ten technical mistakes on the way to the target and still kill it, but at ISU you cannot make one. If you do, the target will have gone! The Station 8 bird at ISU Skeet should be shot in .02 of a second – so there is not a great deal of time.

English Skeet will teach a young person to get his timing right and with correct timing and confidence he will be able to switch to ISU Skeet at a later date with a certain amount of assurance. And once you make the transition from English Skeet and are competent enough to shoot ISU targets reasonably well, you will be able to shoot every type of target from Sporting clays to Trench because you will have mastered the art of gun handling which lies at the heart of all good shooting.

The most important quality in shooting, as in any other sport, is having perfect balance. Hands, eyes and body should move as one with absolute visual concentration on the target. The narrower you are able to keep the visual tunnel between you and the target, the better you will shoot the bird. Timing is dictated by your vision – in other words, the eyes will tell you what to do.

Unfortunately, we have a natural inclination to interfere with what our eyes are telling us; we try to check and make sure that everything is just right instead of allowing the eyes to govern the movement of our hands and body which would then be in perfect time with the target. I have coached hundreds of people over the years and most young people, when told to keep their eye on the target, will move in time with it in the most natural way.

People who have been shooting for a while and have developed bad habits, tend to move their hands quicker than their eyes see the target. They anticipate it, and move the gun before the target is visible and, quite clearly, that is wrong.

If you do anticipate a target and start to move for it before it has appeared, as many people tend to do, it must be incorrect because you are mounting 'blind'. How many times have you seen a shooter shout 'Pull' and bring the gun into his shoulder before the target has appeared? He is moving without knowing the flight of the bird and, consequently, his co-ordination is all wrong.

Nor can I understand shooters who pre-mount their guns. Even though some of them shoot quite successfully in this way, they are inhibiting themselves because what they are doing is not natural and they

English Skeet supremo, Martin Elworthy, a regular winner of the British Open Skeet Championship.

cannot be timing the target correctly. What they should do is call for the target, watch its flight line and move the gun into their shoulder in the direction in which it is travelling. In this way, they will develop excellent timing and hand-to-eye co-ordination. Some shooters call for the bird and mount their guns so fast they are in the wrong position for the flight of the target and they have to swing with the gun in the shoulder. Believe me, it is much easier to swing as you mount and finish the movement with the shot.

Balance is vital and, with any form of shooting, your initial gun movement is the most fundamental and important contribution towards a successful shot. Because they always pre-mount for their targets, some trap shooters are unable to swing and mount

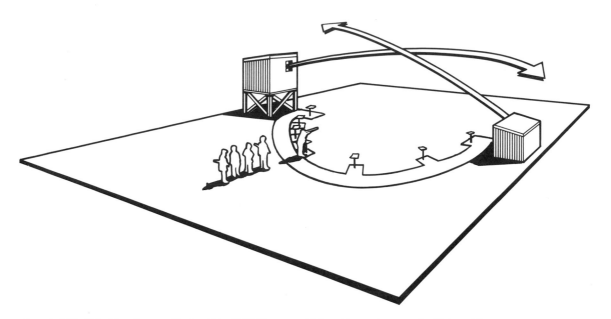

A typical English Skeet layout. Station 8 in ISU Skeet would be mid-way between the high and low houses.

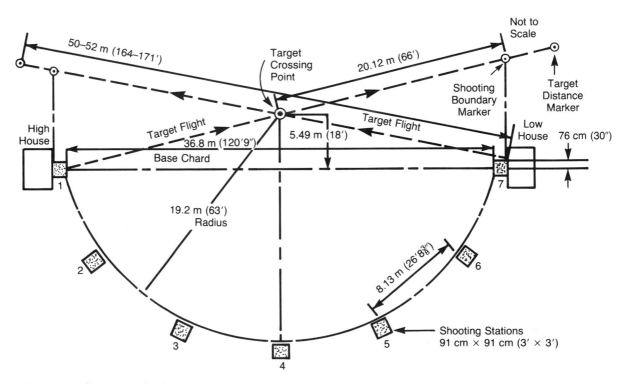

Dimensions for an English Skeet layout.

the gun and would not have the slightest idea how to cope with a crossing target. I think experience of other disciplines would be of great assistance to them and help them to understand how they actually kill the targets.

Another thing which strikes me especially when I watch people shooting Sporting clays, is the very poor footwork of many shooters. They seem very rigid and unwilling to move their feet between one shot and another, and that applies most when they are shooting doubles at FITASC Sporting. Because they never dream of moving their feet between one target and another, which may be going in an opposite direction, they tend to roll off the target trying to get themselves round for

Commonwealth Games ISU Skeet gold medallist, Ken Harman, takes a high-house target.

Joe Neville, Britain's finest ever ISU Skeet shot.

the second bird with their feet rooted to the spot. Good footwork assists a good swing and correct timing follows from that. I am amazed at some of the high scores recorded by shooters who appear to be wearing concrete boots!

There is a lot of debate about so-called Maintained Lead shooting these days. This is a technique where the shooter mounts his gun *in front* of the target instead of swinging through from behind in the traditional way. In Skeet, where the targets fly along a pre-determined trajectory, some shooters have perfected the art of Maintained Lead shooting by calculating to the inch exactly how much they need to lead targets from both high and low houses on the different shooting stations.

I have never used Maintained Lead myself, but in coaching for Skeet shooting, the technique used can depend a little bit on the person one is teaching. You may be coaching three people and two of them will have absolutely no problem at all being taught to swing through the target from behind. For some unknown reason, the third will find it very difficult to move in front of the bird so I would probably teach him Maintained Lead to give him some assistance.

Instinct tells you to shoot directly at the target, and the person I am talking about finds it difficult to move the gun in front of the target before squeezing the trigger. He shoots as his muzzles come to the bird instead of when they are passing it. To begin with, I would teach him to shoot with his gun always in front of the target. That would give him the visual picture that breaks the target.

My technique is simple but effective. I swing the gun from slightly underneath the bird and out in front of it as the gun comes up to my shoulder. As the stock actually comes into my eye and shoulder together, the muzzles are in the place they need to be to kill the target. I always start my swing slightly behind the bird so that the timing of the shot is precise; with Maintained Lead shooting, the slightest misjudgment of pre-determined lead will result in a missed target. Shooting on a swing and coming from behind the target, you can squeeze the trigger in various positions and still kill the bird.

Maintained Lead shooting is really about using plenty of cartridges. If you are prepared to practise it a lot, you can establish an accurate picture of exactly where your barrels should be in relation to the target for a shot, and many people shoot Skeet very successfully with this method. When I am shooting Sporting, I use different methods for different targets. For instance, if I want to shoot a target quickly in a tight situation I will shoot it

Skeet teaches all the qualities essential to good shooting.

with Maintained Lead, with the gun moving in front of the bird all the time. Alternatively, on a distant target I will always move through the bird from behind to give me the correct timing for the shot, exactly as if I were shooting a pheasant in the field.

It is all a question of using the method which is appropriate to the target and there is no doubt that Maintained lead can have advantages in a situation where you have to shoot very quickly at a fast target. When I teach people to shoot, I try to be as flexible as possible, and I always try to teach a method which will suit the style of the person I am instructing. I watch the pupil shoot and then try to improve what he has already got in a way that is particu-

larly suitable to him. There are lots of ways to shoot a bird so do not fall into the trap of believing that there is only one 'correct' shooting method. Experience tells me that it is better to teach a system that will best suit the person who is having a lesson.

I also happen to believe that most people can be taught to shoot to a satisfactory level. Obviously, young people have the best hand-and-eye co-ordination, but there are many people who would see their shooting improve considerably if they took the time to have some lessons with an accomplished coach.

ISU Skeet has not been quite as popular recently in the UK as it used to be but there is evidence that a lot more people are shooting it again. There was a time when many shooting-ground owners were very keen ISU Skeet shots and so tended to install ISU layouts at their grounds. Twenty years ago, there were layouts at Northampton, Bedford, Wimborne, Blandford and Dorchester, Cheddar Valley and Rowarth in Derbyshire and many of those are gone now.

Nevertheless we do have a very good record at international level when you consider that we are purely amateur and our facilities cannot compare with those in the rest of Europe. All the European countries have outstanding Skeet shooters. It does not

matter where you go – Scandinavia, the Eastern bloc, Western Europe – there are superb layouts and excellent shooters. This is because, in these European countries, everyone is either shooting Skeet or Olympic Trap. There are no diversions: if you shoot clays you shoot one or the other, so no talent is every missed.

I can never understand why, in Great Britain, talented shooters do not want to shoot an Olympic discipline. As a sportsman, the Olympic games must be the ultimate goal and I am at a loss to understand why talented shots want to concen-

Shooting is an excellent sport for the handicapped or disabled. This competitor is shooting English Skeet.

trate on non-Olympic disciplines. I have always believed that if our top DTL shooters moved up to Olympic Trench and the leading English Skeet shooters concentrated on ISU Skeet, we would beat the world. And I do not say that lightly. I am convinced we have so much talent in depth that we could sweep all before us. There are people shooting now who could move into the Olympic disciplines and leave the rest of the world standing. I think it is a great pity that this great wealth of talent is not channelled into Olympic Skeet and Trap.

We have some tremendous young shooters coming through at Olympic Trap and, for the first time, we are becoming organized with our training and bringing on young talent. We have weekly training days for them and we are starting to get ISU Skeet organized along the same lines. At Skeet, we have shooters as young as eleven who are putting in some phenomenal scores for their age and who do not consider the training sessions to be a drudgery. We have reached the stage where they want to be together regularly to practise and discuss the sport, and that attitude augurs well for the future.

If we can maintain this progress and interest, I am optimistic that we will be able to develop talent in depth at last and really compete on the world stage. There is no doubt that we have the shooters. It is up to us to make sure that they do not slip through the net.

7 Automatic Ball Trap

By James Birkett-Evans

James Birkett-Evans is fast emerging as one of Britain's most consistent Olympic Trap shots. He is a regular member of the Great Britain Team and won a silver medal for Wales in the pairs event at the 1990 Commonwealth Games in New Zealand. In 1989, he was the British ABT champion with a score of 186 out of 200.

I took the hardest imaginable route into clay shooting: straight into Olympic Trench, and there cannot be any discipline more certain to demolish the confidence of a newcomer to the sport. At my first attempt on an OT layout, I hit only two targets out of twenty-five and there were other equally disheartening outings before my scores gradually started to improve.

What was certainly my most humiliating

ABT is an ideal preparation for OT.

70

moment in those early days came in Canada when I confidently entered an OT competition and, in front of a fairly large crowd, killed one bird and missed all the others! I suppose a lot of people would have given up there and then, but I was more determined than ever to succeed and, when I returned to the UK, I started shooting regularly at the North Wales Shooting School and Garlands SG in the Midlands. There, I studied the technique of top shooters and later had regular coaching with excellent teachers like Peter Croft and Peter Boden. Since then, it has been a long hard grind to reach the level I have attained today and, like all shooters, I am still learning every time I pick up my gun.

The point I am making is that there are no short cuts to good shooting. I know now that I would have been far better equipped to tackle Trench targets if I had taken the conventional route and shot some of the other trap disciplines first.

There is no doubt that ABT is an ideal preparation for OT: the shooter has full use of the gun, plenty of straight going-away birds and difficult angled shots, especially on the outside pegs. Because it only requires one trap, ABT is much simpler to stage than Olympic Trap. Consequently, many local grounds have Ball Trap as well as DTL, so you should not have much difficulty in finding a ground where you can shoot it. As far as I am concerned, there is another outstanding reason to shoot ABT: you can represent your country at the discipline, which is surely a great incentive to be successful.

ABT is shot by a squad of six shooters, each of whom shoots at one target from one of five pegs before moving to his right to shoot again from the next peg. The sequence is completed when each shooter has shot twenty-five targets, five from each peg. An experienced squad will move fairly quickly with each shooter mounting

his gun, shooting and preparing to move to his right in a steady, uninterrupted rhythm.

A common error made by many shooters when they first attempt ABT is to mount their gun and watch the mark on the trap-house where they believe the target will appear when they call for it. But you do not watch the bonnet when you are driving your car, you look out ahead, and that is exactly what you should do when you are shooting. The distance you look out from the trap depends how high the stock on your gun is. The higher the stock, the more rib you will see and the further you should look out. With a flat-shooting gun, you should be looking quite close to the mark. I mount my gun on the top of the trap-house and look out over the barrels in a kind of soft focus, not concentrating my vision on any particular spot so that I will see the target as soon as it appears and in whichever direction it is going.

Once you have called for the bird, you should let it go until you see it clearly before you move your gun and that often means holding your swing for a split second. When the target first emerges from the trap it will appear as a streak. Train yourself to wait until the streak has become a clearly defined clay right in the centre of your vision before swinging on to it.

Some people, and Ian Peel is one of them, can watch an Olympic Trench target for 10 yards before moving onto it and still kill it far quicker every single time than someone who moves with the bird the moment it emerges from the trap. This is because, if you move your gun with the clay, you tend to move at the same speed as the target, so when you squeeze the trigger you miss behind. However, if you let the target go for a few yards so that you have to come from behind it, you will naturally accelerate to catch it. In other

Look out ahead of the trap-house at ABT.

words, you will instinctively swing faster than the target is moving. Squeeze the trigger as your barrels reach it and you should kill it. It takes considerable discipline to train yourself to allow the target to go in this way. Your natural reaction will be to chase it with your gun the moment it appears, but if you do you will certainly miss more times than you hit it!

Once you have started to record respectable scores at ABT, you may want to try Universal Trench and then move on to Olympic Trap, as many of our leading shooters have. If you are determined, there

is absolutely no reason why you should not succeed, but, as I said earlier, you will get a great deal of satisfaction if you decide that ABT is the discipline for you and a place in your national team could be your inspiration.

Shooting is a superb and friendly sport but it embraces so many variables that it can bring you great joy or heartbreak when you are trying to win a shoot. To be really successful you have to reach the stage where it is second nature to you to do everything absolutely right every single time you prepare to shoot a bird. Somebody once said to me that if you put 100 clays on the ground in a row and hit them with a hammer, the likelihood is that you would miss one – and that really sums up how much is involved in doing everything perfectly every time without exception.

Shooting really is an unforgiving sport. You can powder ten clays with your first barrel, then make one tiny mistake and the eleventh bird is gone – and you suddenly find yourself worse off than the shooter next to you who has only chipped every target with his second barrel. Sometimes you wonder where the justice is.

So go out and try ABT and be prepared for setbacks and the frequent days when nothing goes right. But I guarantee you will enjoy it and the path from the local Ball Trap layout to Trench, and perhaps the Olympic games, is a well-trodden one. It is certainly worth thinking about.

8 Women and Shooting

By Denise Eyre

Denise Eyre started clay shooting in 1980, mainly concentrating on Skeet and English Sporting. In 1984, she switched to FITASC Sporting and has since been Ladies' World Champion three times and European Champion on two occasions. In 1990, she won the FITASC World Cup. Denise also enjoys shooting Olympic Trench. Her husband Tony is a keen FITASC shot and the couple run a shooting ground specializing in English and FITASC Sporting at Glossop in Derbyshire.

Although more and more women are coming into competitive clay shooting every season, their numbers are only a fraction of what we would see if there was a concerted effort to offer them just a little encouragement. If you think that sounds ungrateful coming from someone who has travelled the world shooting at the highest level, perhaps I should emphasize that without the support of my husband and the confidence of sponsors who have stuck by me through thick and thin, I am sure I would never have been so successful.

I am not suggesting that there is discrimination against women in shooting, because there is not. But it is discouraging to consider that those women who succeed do so in spite of the way the sport is run rather than because of it. There are very real disadvantages for women at the sport's grass roots where many small grounds and their members fail to make even the slightest attempt to welcome or encourage them. It stands to reason that if we do not persuade more women to participate in shooting, a great pool of latent talent will remain untapped. After all, it is from local shooting grounds that the champions of tomorrow will emerge.

Women really are decisively outnumbered wherever shoots are held and the shortage of female competitors is not confined to the UK by any means. The 1990 World FITASC Championships held in France attracted a record entry of more than 700 shooters with competitors from France, Italy, Belgium, Cyprus, Holland, Austria.

Sarah Bayley, one of Britain's finest women FITASC prospects.

Concentration as Denise Eyre prepares to call for a target.

Switzerland and even the USA and Australia. Out of that impressive multi-national entry there were only thirty-six women, so the attitudes that inhibit the development and enthusiasm of women shooters here in Great Britain are clearly just as deeply entrenched and difficult to surmount in other countries.

The problems at home arise at local level, at the small shooting grounds which do not make any effort to attract women competitors. Many of them do not organize ladies' classes, so, if they do participate, women pay the same entry fee as men and have very little chance of winning anything. If shoot organizers took the trouble to stage a class for ladies whenever there was more than one woman shooting, it would at least be an incentive for them to take part.

All the blame cannot be laid on the clubs. Most women do not get the opportunity to shoot because their husbands or boyfriends never invite them to have a go – you only have to look at the male-dominated entry at most Sunday morning events to see what I mean. I am extremely fortunate in that my husband Tony had always given me tremendous encouragement but a lot of men seem to regard the shooting ground as an all-male preserve and are very reluctant to invite women along.

If they do ask wives or girlfriends to accompany them, more often than not they frighten them off by failing to give them proper instruction. It is absolutely pointless to push a gun into a woman's hands and tell her when to pull the trigger. The chances are she will end up flat on her back from recoil and never want to shoot again. This actually happened to a woman I know and she was absolutely terrified by the experience because she had not been warned exactly what would happen when she fired the gun. I later spent a lot of time with her, patiently explaining how she should stand and mount her gun correctly and now she has become interested, bought a gun and shoots regularly.

I am sure more women would catch the shooting bug if they were invited to a ground and given a thorough explanation of what to expect before they fired a single shot. Now that the lighter 1-ounce loads are compulsory in most disciplines and therefore widely available, there is no reason at all for women to fear recoil.

Nor do they have to be built like Eastern European shot-putters to handle a gun sucessfully. Most women shooters on the international circuit and certainly in Great Britain are of only average build and definitely very feminine. I am 5 feet 2 inches, and weigh 8 stone and have absolutely no difficulty in handling a Browning shotgun, which weighs just over 8 pounds.

Most women shooters are definitely very feminine.

Having said that, I do make a very real effort to keep as fit as possible and work out in the gym most lunch-times to build up my stamina and I also do weight training.

As in any sport, it is essential to keep as fit as possible and I have certainly felt the benefit of my regular work-outs during gruelling three-day FITASC competitions. I am convinced that physical fitness also improves mental approach and concentration is vital in a sport where one missed target can mean the difference between success and failure.

It really illustrates how few women shooters have come into the sport in recent years when you consider that when I started to shoot FITASC in 1984 the outstanding woman shooter was Anthea Hillyer. Anthea has now been World Champion six times and I have won it on three occasions. In the 1990 Championships in France, Anthea won again and I was second. We almost seem to take the title in turns, year in and year out. I do not mean this in a conceited way, for, as satisfying as it is to keep winning, I cannot help feeling it is time we were being challenged at the highest level by some new young women.

Recently, there have been indications that several young Britons like Sarah

Anthea Hillyer, six times women's World FITASC Champion.

The British women's FITASC team in the 1990 European championships. Edith Barnes, Tina Merrick and Sarah Bayley.

Bayley and Ruth Leah are coming through at international level, so perhaps things are about to change at last. Ruth won the European FITASC Championship in 1990 and Sarah was third in the world as well as winning the British and English Open Sporting competitions.

Any woman reading this who fancies shooting and is not getting the necessary encouragement from the man in her life can obtain a list of qualified coaches from the CPSA and take herself off for a lesson; there is sure to be a coach within striking distance, wherever you live. Then enter some local shoots to get the feel of

competition. You will be surprised how appealing the sport becomes once you start breaking clays!

Once you have gained some confidence, try the different disciplines and decide which one appeals to you most. I think there is a lot to be said for shooters becoming proficient at another discipline before devoting themselves exclusively to Sporting. I started my career in 1980 shooting Skeet and there is no doubt that the grounding I had in that discipline has benefited me ever since. Disciplines like Skeet and Down the Line teach you steady gun mounting and a smooth swing.

Sharon McLoughlin, also aiming for the top at FITASC.

Many of our top male sporting shooters excelled in one of the disciplines before switching to Sporting. A. J. Smith was an outstanding Olympic Trench shot and George Digweed and Mickey Rouse were both top-class Skeet shooters, so there are clear advantages in mastering one discipline or another before devoting yourself to Sporting shooting, if indeed that is what you want to do.

If you graduate from DTL and become excited by the challenge of Olympic Trench, you may decide to stick to that; and bear in mind that as its name indicates it is an Olympic discipline so there is always the ultimate goal of eventually representing Great Britain in the Olympic games – there is a tremendous incentive to succeed if ever there was one.

Shooting is an exceptional sport for men or women and, if you have the slightest interest in it, I would unhesitatingly recommend you to try it. Because I have been successful, I have been fortunate enough to travel all over the world in competition and visited countries I probably would never have gone to in the normal way. It has given me a storehouse of wonderful memories and a tremendous social life and friends throughout the world. I firmly believe that if more women entered the sport, it would not be long before we were challenging men on an equal footing.

This lady shooter is doing everything right and concentrating hard on the target.

Anthea Hillyer was eighth overall in the World Championships in Australia a few years ago, and I finished eighth overall in the EC Grand Prix in Belgium in 1989. When you consider how few women took part in these competitions, these were incredible feats.

So let us hope that women start getting the encouragement they deserve. It can only benefit the sport of clay shooting – if not the men!

79

9 Basic Clay Shooting Tuition

By Ian Coley

Ian Coley has shot more disciplines at international level than any other competitor. He has represented England at Sporting, DTL, ABT and Olympic Trap and has been a member of Great Britain teams for OT, ABT and Universal Trench. He has won the British ABT and the English UT Championships as well as the English All Round. Ian, who is manager of the Great Britain UT and OT teams, owns a gunshop in Cheltenham and runs a renowned shooting school at Chatcome Estate, near Cheltenham. He is a Fellow of the Institute of Clay Shooting Instructors.

Before I describe the mistakes that are common to most novice shooters, some of you will probably find it reassuring if I make it absolutely clear at the outset that, in all my years of coaching, I have never had a hopeless case.

If the newcomer has confidence in his coach, and is willing to listen and learn and

Keep your movements smooth as the gun comes up into your face.

practise, he can certainly be taught to shoot to a very reasonable level of competence. However, there is one major problem facing both novice and instructor at the beginning. I am referring to the number of self-appointed coaches at local shoots who dispense advice with the best possible intention but only create great confusion in the mind of the beginner. These people may be quite correct in identifying where a shooter is missing a particular target, but usually they do not have the experience to pinpoint the cause. And even in the rare cases when they can see why and where he is missing, the are not able to explain to the shooter how to correct it. Sadly, their well-intentioned advice can prove a major setback for people.

If you are having a course of lessons and run into this type of instant 'instruction' just try to ignore it. It can only serve to cause you a great deal of bewilderment.

AIMING AND POINTING

Without any doubt, the most common mistakes made by the majority of novices is 'aiming' the gun, instead of having the confidence to look at the target with only 'muzzle awareness'. Time and time again, I see pupils focus on the foresight at the end of their barrels and proceed to aim the gun, instead of point it.

To illustrate the difference between aiming and pointing, I suggest the pupil carries out the following simple exercise:

Point the index finger at an imaginary target with both eyes open and concentrate on that target. This will allow the required 'awareness' of the finger and nothing more. The target will be in perfect focus.

Concentrate on the end of the finger, the equivalent of the gun's foresight, and the 'target' will become distorted and out of focus. It is a vivid and practical demonstration of the difference between pointing and aiming – and it is something the novice can try anywhere at any time.

I can tell immediately when a pupil is looking at the gun's foresight instead of the target because I can see the gun barrels juddering, searching for the clay, which is not clearly visible to the shooter because he is looking down at the barrels and the foresight.

Aiming the gun is initially a particular problem with going-away targets. Because such a small amount of gun movement is required for a basic going-away bird, the pupil automatically focuses on the foresight instead of on the area where the target will appear.

Many novices also tend to 'rainbow' on crossing targets. This means that they bring the gun up in an arc and then swing down again to find the target. Once again, this is the result of looking at the end of the barrels instead of letting the eyes follow the line of the bird.

I cannot stress enough the importance of 'muzzle awareness', nothing more nor less. It is essential to smooth and efficient shooting.

The shooter should stand with his feet 9 inches to a foot apart, with the toes at one o'clock and three o'clock.

Do not lift your head off the stock . . .

THE IMPORTANCE OF LEAD

When a person has just started shooting, 90 per cent of targets are missed behind. Although I teach people to start their swing behind the target and to accelerate through it, most of them still tend to shoot straight at the bird. They do not have the confidence to swing through naturally, without checking. So when a novice comes to me for a course of lessons, I start by explaining the principles of shotgun shooting and the significance of lead, which is the distance the *moving* and accelerating barrels must be ahead of the target in order to kill it. I emphasize to the pupil the importance of being as natural as possible, of letting things happen rather than forcing them. If you can be natural, rather than tense and rushed, your shooting will be far less inhibited. Ideally, the gun should be an extension of the shooter's body.

Too many novices try to shoot a crossing target quickly, without allowing their eyes to judge its distance and speed naturally. I always stress to them the absolute necessity of mounting behind the target and accelerating fluently through it to a given lead picture before squeezing the trigger while continuing the swing. Novices tend to stop and start the gun as they swing, never believing in themselves enough to get in front of the target. And if they do move ahead of the bird and pull the trigger, they are inclined to stop swinging, which also results in a miss behind.

At this early stage, I am a great believer in the use of snap caps. They are dummy cartridges placed in the barrel chamber which enable the trigger to be pulled without damaging the firing mechanism. By using snap caps, the pupil does not have recoil to anticipate and I am able to establish his sight picture, his perception of the gun in relation to the target, before letting him actually fire a cartridge.

All novices tend to be tense and nervous when they are firing their first shot, and this reflects in their leading arm becoming far too stiff at the joint. Others tend to grip the gun far too tightly. If necessary, I will assist the pupil to establish the correct sight picture by standing behind him and helping to pull the gun through the line and in front of the target before telling him precisely when to squeeze the trigger. There is absolutely no point in firing a cartridge when one is obviously nowhere near the target, but once a satisfactory sight picture has been established, the pupil can attempt to kill a target with a real cartridge.

. . . keep it in the correct position.

*I am against novice's shooting off the back foot.
It can have a bad effect on their balance.*

PATTERN AND SHOT STRING

I believe it is very helpful to a novice who is missing targets behind if I take the trouble to explain pattern and shot string. It helps to give him a clear mental picture of what actually happens when he pulls the trigger.

First, I demonstrate the spread of pellets on a pattern plate, but even more important, in my opinion, is an explanation of shot string. I describe the way cartridge pellets travel in a column perhaps 5 or 6 feet in length and and point out that even if you exaggerate the lead necessary to kill a target, the chances are that you will hit it with some part of the shot string. Pupils

are then encouraged to overestimate the lead picture they believe is correct: I tell them to try to miss the target in front and find that they still kill the clay with the back end of the shot string.

ANTICIPATION

Another very common error, especially with a close going-away bird, is anticipation of the target. The shooter hears the trap and, before the clay has appeared, has moved his gun assuming he knows where the target will go.

It probably sounds as if I am stating the obvious when I say that it is vitally important for the shooter to see the target before there is any gun movement but you would be surprised how many top-flight competitors fall into this trap and miss birds by anticipation. It is an error which is by no means confined to the beginner!

FOOTWORK

For a right-handed shooter, I always teach the accepted stance, with the feet 9 inches to a foot apart and the toes at one o'clock and three o'clock. However, I do not believe in the old-fashioned method of having a straight line across the heels to where the shooter is going to break the target. I always like to see a slight angle towards the left of the straight line.

Also I am most insistent that learners shoot off the front foot. I do not agree with novices shooting off the back foot for any type of target, including driven. Eighty per cent of people shoot off the front foot, and they can start to use the back foot later for certain shots once they have learned to shoot correctly. Shooting off the back foot too soon can have a detrimental effect on their balance.

BARREL LENGTH

For a beginner, I would always recommend 28-inch barrels and, if the person I am teaching is of normal physical build, I would use an Over-and-Under.

Women can be just as proficient as men at shooting but, at the start, there is a particular problem in overcoming their inherent nervousness of recoil. When I am teaching a woman who is strong enough to handle the weight of a Sporting 12-bore shotgun, I always advocate a 12-bore instead of a 20-bore. Because a 20-bore tends to be lighter, the recoil can be quite vicious so I would suggest using the 12-bore with a low recoil shell.

A. J. Smith's relaxed shooting style makes even the fastest target appear slow. He is an outstanding natural shot, one of the best in the world.

This lady is using a semi-automatic shotgun. Many women find them lighter to handle and there is less recoil.

CHOKES

There is a lot of nonsense talked about chokes. I believe that multichoke shotguns are bad for novices because people get far too involved in worrying about which choke they are using instead of concentrating on correct shooting technique. They walk off a stand, having missed the targets, and blame the chokes. In fact, that is not the reason they have missed at all; they blame the chokes purely to obscure their own lack of ability. Learners should use open-choked guns, and by that I mean quarter-quarter or quarter-half; do not make the mistake of constantly changing chokes and ignore all the rubbish people talk on the subject.

Another very common cause of missed targets of all kinds is the tendency for many shooters to lift their heads off the stock as they shoot, which instantly destroys their sight picture. Usually, it is the result of lack of confidence, a wish to make sure they are on the bird, which causes this fault but sometimes it can be the outcome of shooting with a very low-combed gun.

In this chapter, I have tried to explain just a few of the most common mistakes committed by novices. Descriptions of them all and how to rectify them have filled many books.

Shooting is an art and there is no substitute for good tuition. If you are considering taking up the sport, book a course of lessons with a qualified coach.

Finally, always bear in mind what I tell my pupils: the clay you are shooting now is the most important one of all. Forget the one that has just gone, and do not even think about the one that is to follow. Concentrate on the target you have called for – after all, you can only shoot it once. And in a competition, that concentration could make the vital difference between winning or losing!

10 Organizing a Championship Shoot

By Dai Jones

Dai Jones has been an enthusiastic game shooter since he was a boy. For many years he had a gun-shop in Shrewsbury and, in 1981, he became proprietor of the West Midlands Shooting Ground at Hodnet, Shropshire, where he has staged many major clay-shooting events, including the British Open Sporting Championship and the World Sporting Jubilee, to celebrate the 60th anniversary of the CPSA.

National championship shoots attract more entries every year. It is now a regular occurrence for more than 1,500 competitors to take part in competitions like the British Open Sporting Championship, and the natural consequence of such a large entry is intense pressure and literally months of hard work for the ground where the event is to be held.

It is not just a question of ensuring that the targets are sufficiently testing and enjoyable for every class of shooter, although that must always be a predominant consideration. It is also making absolutely certain that every component necessary for successfully handling 300 guns a day for almost a week has been anticipated and prepared for.

Team-work is essential. Every single person connected in any way with staging the event – the administration staff, the referees, the trappers, the scorers, the caterers – must have been correctly briefed, and know exactly what is required of them. When we staged the World Sporting Jubilee at Hodnet in 1988, our full-time staff prepared for months beforehand, and

during the event we had a team of seventy people working flat out every day to make it a success. So many people now want to shoot the major competitions, and are prepared to travel such great distances from all over the UK and abroad to do so, that events have to be organized meticulously.

Targets are the first thing to exercise my mind. I think about them constantly for many months before an event and spend hours working out various combinations, setting up imaginary stands. Because I have always had a great love of game shooting, I try whenever possible to ensure that targets simulate the flight of gamebirds. They must be within clean killing distance of a shotgun (a maximum of 40 yards at the point where they should be shot) and presented in such a way that they actually test the art of shooting. In my opinion, many Sporting clay shooters are becoming mechanical in the way they shoot, mainly because they tend to encounter the same type of target, week in week out.

In a 100-bird championship shoot, I like to see a winning score of about 90, and that means that I must make sure that two of the ten stands test the ability of the top shooters to the very limit. They must be stands where they will see targets they have never shot before; where they will have to work very hard for a respectable score; where their ability to 'read' targets is tested; where the fine art of shooting is thoroughly examined.

I do not like targets that are thrown as simultaneous pairs, but I am fond of good on-report birds and following pairs. The combination of some targets, which as singles may be quite simple, can make them very difficult. They will test the shooter's control, footwork and self-

discipline and catch many people out in the process.

The low pheasant is one of my favourite targets here at Hodnet. It is relatively high and about 35 yards out, and originates from a trap above and to the left of the shooter. If you were able to watch the target from above, you would see the clay leave the trap and curl back in an arc to the right of the shooter. To the shooter, however, it appears to be a straight crosser, and it is those shooters who are able to read its flight-line who are successful.

I try to deceive the shooter by presenting targets that are not what they seem: the oncoming bird which is just off-centre and

The score-board, always a point of interest, outside the clubhouse at Hodnet.

The scorer crouches to establish beyond doubt whether this is a hit or miss.

curling; the simultaneous pair of teal off different traps, simulating how real teal get up, with one slightly quicker than the other. This type of target is especially difficult for the shooter who has a preconceived notion of what he is seeing.

As I said earlier, the targets are only one part of a successful shoot. We are proud of the fact that when the British Open was held at Hodnet, it was the first time that there were qualified referees on every stand. More and more professional people, who are used to handling staff, are becoming referees. If they can be authoritative, without being officious, they can be a tremendous asset to the event. Shooters will not usually argue with the decisions of a referee who exudes authority. And never let it be forgotten that a referee must shoot every target!

There is another essential qualification for a successful referee: a sense of humour. It is helpful, too, to have trapping experience and a working knowledge of gun mechanisms, and I like to see referees on first name terms with their trappers. Unfortunately, some referees and shooters tend to forget that, without trappers, there is no shoot.

Trappers should be sensible and responsible, and I firmly believe that an intelligent trapper is far better any time than an

Try to deceive a shooter by presenting targets which are not what they seem.

automatic trap. Because of the outstanding natural features here, most of the targets come from a source that cannot be seen by the shooter and, if the wind changes slightly, the clays can start hitting the trees and breaking. A good trapper can be invaluable in these circumstances, making the fine adjustments that an automatic trap cannot make.

They must be well briefed and well trained, and have a rapport with the referee on their stand. Our trappers always go out in the morning with a kit which includes gloves, ear plugs, first-aid equipment, fly repellent and protective goggles – and a Mars bar!

Because they all have their favourite traps at Hodnet, they get to know the 'feel'

of their traps and can tell if something is not quite right. It can contribute considerably to your peace of mind if you know that, on each stand, there are sensible and reliable trappers who have an understanding with a dependable referee. It is one thing less to worry about.

It is important that when a relief team takes over, there is an overlap so that the targets are sent on the same trajectories and the referees know that this is correct. In case of trap breakdowns, we always have two maintenance men available throughout an event in radio contact with the office.

There must also be an experienced staff on duty in the shoot office, where teamwork is essential. They will not only be

This shooting stand is in beautiful natural surroundings.

dealing with shooters checking in and others handing in their completed cards but a thousand and one other enquiries. Again, when the British Open was held here, our staff were able to provide full results in every class just thirty-four minutes after the final card was handed in, a tribute to their organization and team-work.

At the end of each day, we ask the trappers to clear up their empty clay boxes and help to pick up spent cartridges. Then we send teams out to collect the day's rubbish and, when the first shooters go out on to the ground the next morning, they would never know that any shooting had taken place the previous day.

The horn is used to tell the trapper when the shooter has called for his target.

When you are setting up a shoot, you must always be certain you are doing so in the safest way possible. Oncoming targets are the most sensitive from the point of view of safety, so the organizers must always ensure that shooters and the crowd are conducted into a narrow channel from the side to allow clay and shoot fall-out behind.

I also like to have barriers between the crowd and the shooter and referee, so the referee has complete control of the shooting area and does not have to worry about what is happening behind him. It is also important to let the police, your neighbours and local authority know that you are staging a big event. If you take the trouble to keep everyone concerned in the picture, it can create a lot of goodwill.

There is no doubt that organizing a national championship is hard work, but it can also be very satisfying. I like to think we have got the running of the events mastered here at Hodnet. My ambition now is to put on a major shoot where every single target of the competition is different. That really would be something special – and I am quite sure that we shall be able to do it in the not-too-distant future.

11 Other Disciplines

There are several other forms of clay-pigeon shooting, some of them derivatives of the various trap disciplines and others based on sporting targets. The newest of them is Double Trap, devised by the ISU as the third Olympic shotgun event and first introduced in 1988.

Originally, targets were launched from two traps 1 metre apart on a layout similar to that for Olympic Trap. The left-hand trap was fixed and threw a straight target,

'They said this was a foxy shoot – but this is ridiculous.'

but the right-hand one was auto-angling and the target varied in angle and height.

One of the main objections to Double Trap in this form was the inclusion of the oscillating trap which made it possible for one shooter to receive a series of difficult double combinations while another had much easier targets. This was contrary to the set-up in other Olympic disciplines where each shooter receives exactly the same targets, although not necessarily in the same order. There was such a lack of interest in the new discipline because of its difficulty and unfairness that the ISU went back to the drawing-board.

Under the new rules for the discipline, the auto-angling trap has been dispensed with and three fixed traps used, the equivalent of numbers seven, eight and nine on an OT layout and two, three and four at UT. The left-hand trap may be set at between 0 and 15 degrees to the left; the right-hand trap between the same limits to the right and the centre trap 5 degrees either side of centre.

The new rules eliminate the unfairness of the original version in that each shooter receives the same target distribution but in a different sequence. Only time will tell, however, whether the new Double Trap will recover from its false start to attract shooters as much as the other trap disciplines.

There has, of course, long been another double-target event in clay shooting in the United States and the United Kingdom. Double Rise is a variation of DTL where two targets are thrown simultaneously

A Down the Line squad in action.

instead of one. The shooter is allowed one shot at each target and scores five points for killing both clays and two points for killing one of a pair.

Single Barrel is also a derivative of DTL and is a competition where only one shot per target is permissible.

In Handicap-by-Distance, the shooter is handicapped according to his ability, by standing at a greater distance from the trap. The maximum handicap distance in Great Britain is 23 yards and in the USA, 27 yards.

ZZ Target has probably the smallest but most enthusiastic following of any form of clay shooting. The target is a two- or three-bladed plastic propeller with a detachable centre which requires special release equipment. One of five traps in front of the shooter releases the target on call, and the competitor may fire two shots at each target. The centre must be knocked out and the broken target fall inside a small fence if it is to count. In Great Britain, ZZ is almost exclusively confined to the south of England but in France it is extremely popular and large sums of money can be won by the sport's professional shooters.

Starshot, designed by Scottish shooter David Maxwell, was specifically devised

Blow the smoke from the barrels and reload for the next target.

for television, and a Starshot competition generated considerable interest when it was shown as a series on BBC2. Targets have to be broken as they are thrown up a semi-circular frame; kills in certain segments score higher than others.

There is no doubt that the hysteria and adverse publicity for all forms of shooting that was generated in the aftermath of the Hungerford massacre kept Starshot off the screen after the BBC2 series. Given the interest it created, however, it is surprising that Channel 4 or one of the satellite TV sports channels have not moved in to televise it since.

There are several permanent Starshot layouts in the UK, and mobile layouts visit many country fairs each summer.

Pro-trap is especially popular with many leading Sporting and FITASC shooters. Traps release clays in a computerized sequence so that a shooter has twenty-five different targets from one position. Again, this is very popular as an adjunct to a Sporting shoot at game and country fairs.

A well-organized Flush can be a great deal of fun to participate in. Two- or three-man teams are thrown perhaps fifty driven targets in a continuous stream after calling for the first bird. It requires very fast loading and shooting by all the team members to record a high score. The winning team is often the one with the best tactics (left-hand shooter takes left-hand targets etc.) and the ability to spot the bird that is getting away while someone is reloading.

Appendix I

FIREARMS AND THE LAW

By Tony Hoare

A series of shooting incidents in the late 1980s, and especially the Hungerford massacre in which sixteen people were shot dead, led to considerable public disquiet about the ownership of guns. This culminated in a sustained and successful campaign for more stringent firearms legislation. The result was the introduction of the Firearms (Amendment) Act 1988, which imposed new controls relating to the ownership of guns in Great Britain.

Exactly how stiffening the rules on gun ownership for law-abiding shooters was ex-

A pattern plate, used to indicate the pattern being thrown by your gun and cartridge.

pected to achieve a reduction in armed crime has never been satisfactorily explained. Nevertheless, the new Act made important changes to the classification of some types of gun and affected the authorization required for lawful possession, purchase, acquisition or sale of weapons.

One of the main problems for Sporting shooters arose out of the way individual police forces interpreted Home Office guide-lines for the security of guns in the home, a new and integral condition of the Act. Unfortunately, the Home Office did not issue a statutory definition of security and different police forces have applied different standards. Some demand Shotgun Certificate holders to have very rigid security arrangements, not only in relation to shotguns within a house; some also insisted that the house itself be additionally protected with window locks and deadlocks.

At the other extreme, some forces are happy if the guns are dismantled and simply locked away out of sight. Individual police officers from the same force have even been known to disagree over security requirements in the absence of clear guide-lines. The differences of opinion obviously created great confusion for shooters, and have continued to do so.

The British Association for Shooting and Conservation (BASC), the CPSA and other shooting organizations made strong representations to the Home Office, individual police forces, MPs and the Firearms Consultative Committee over interpretation of the guide-lines. And in the absence of unambiguous guidance from the Home Office, the CPSA laid down its own recommendations in a booklet, *Shotguns and the Law*. However, even these were not enough to satisfy some police forces. The CPSA advised:

Paul Cockle has graduated from Down the Line to shoot all the trap disciplines.

Although there is no actual requirements in law for the owner of a shotgun to keep the weapon in a security cabinet, it is thoroughly recommended by the CPSA.

The cabinet should be made in steel of at least 2mm thickness (14 swg) with two separate hidden five-lever locks and with welded hinges and concealed pivots.

The cabinet should be bolted securely to the wall and floor from the inside of the cabinet, ensuring that there is no gap between the cabinet and the wall to which it is fixed. A corner of a room is a good position – the cabinet can be bolted to both walls and the floor.

It may also be sensible to check with the Crime Prevention Officer or the Firearms Department of the police authority in whose area you live, to establish the level of security they require. A steel cabinet is clearly a good idea, whatever their minimum stipulations.

The main requirements of the Firearms (Amendment) Act 1988 are summarized below. More detailed information can be obtained from your local police headquarters.

Criteria for the Issueing of a Shotgun Certificate

A Chief Officer of Police will *not* grant a shotgun certificate if:

(a) he is not satisfied that the applicant can possess a shotgun without danger to public safety or to the peace;

(b) he is satisfied that the applicant does not have a good reason for possessing, purchasing or acquiring a gun (examples of good reasons are sporting or competition purposes, the shooting of vermin and some situations where the gun is not intended for use, such as if it is an heirloom or part of a collection);

(c) he has reason to believe the applicant is prohibited from possessing a shotgun.

Section 1 – Firearms Certificate

This is required for:

(a) a smooth-bore gun with a bore of more than 1 inch diameter;

(b) a smooth-bore revolver (9mm-rim fire or muzzle loading only);

(c) a smooth-bore gun with a fixed magazine capable of holding more than two cartridges;

(d) a smooth-bore gun with a barrel length less than 24 inches.

Note:

(1) You may not possess, purchase or acquire any of these weapons unless you have already obtained a Firearm Certificate from your local police. They will not issue a Certificate unless they are satisfied that you have a good reason for having it, that public safety is not endangered and that you are fit to be entrusted. The Chief Officer of Police may impose conditions and may revoke a Certificate.

(2) If you gain possession of any of these weapons without a Certificate you are liable on conviction to imprisonment or a fine or both.

(3) You may not sell, lend or give any of these weapons to anyone who has not got a Firearm Certificate.

John Dyson has been a top Sporting shot for many years.

(4)   You may not lend, or make a gift of any of these weapons to a child under fourteen years old; and you may not sell them to anyone under seventeen.

Section 2 – Shotgun Certificate

This is required for:
(a)   a smooth-bore gun with a bore not exceeding 2 inches in diameter;
(b)   a smooth-bore gun which is not a revolver;
(c)   a smooth-bore gun with a fixed magazine capable of holding not more than two cartridges;
(d) a smooth-bore gun with a barrel length of 24 inches or more (not being an airgun).

Section 5 – Prohibited Weapons

You may not possess or acquire:
(a)   a smooth-bore gun which is capable of 'burst firing' (firing more than once for a single pull of the trigger);
(b)   self-loading smooth-bore guns which have a barrel of less than 24 inches in length or an overall length of less than 40 inches;
(c)   pump-action smooth-bore guns which have a barrel of less than 24 inches in length or an overall length of less than 40 inches;
(d)   smooth-bore revolvers;
(e)   a converted shotgun that has since become a prohibited weapon under the new laws.

Applying for a Shotgun Certificate

(a)   All Shotgun Certificates issued on or after 1 July 1989 will bear a photograph of the holder. All first-time applicants who apply on or after this date will complete a new-style application form.

(b)   The Certificates contain a detailed description of all guns held on the Certificate, including any identification numbers. You will therefore need to provide this information on the new Shotgun Certificate application form.

(c)   A safe-keeping condition appears on all Shotgun Certificates. This demands two distinct levels of security to ensure safe custody of the guns.

Renewal of Existing Certificates

If you already hold a Shotgun Certificate, you do not need to apply to renew until shortly before its expiry date.

Transfer and Sale of Shotguns

(a)   From 1 July 1989, requirements concerning the transfer of shotguns between private individuals came into force.

(b)   Transfer in this context means sale, letting on hire, giving as a gift or lending for more than seventy-two hours. They do not apply where the person acquiring the gun is a registered firearms dealer, or someone exempt from the need to hold a Certificate.

A dropping pair of clays crossing in front of the shooter can be very difficult. There is a tendency to shoot above them.

This is an excellent spot for a Sporting stand. The trees and water help to simulate game shooting.

(c) When both parties to the transfer hold Certificates issued or renewed on or after 1 July 1989, the following requirements apply:

(i) A person tranferring a shotgun must enter details of the gun on the new holder's Certificate. Within seven days of the transaction, he must also send a notice of the transaction to the Chief Officer of Police who issued his Shotgun Certificate. If the person transferring the shotgun is exempt from the need to hold a Certificate, he should notify details of the transaction to the Chief Constable who issued the Certificate to the gun's new holder.

(ii) A person who acquires a shotgun must send a note of the transaction taking place to the Chief Constable who issued his Certificate.

This left-handed shooter is using his right hand to swing the gun in front of the target before shooting it.

Gun down, out of the shoulder, at FITASC, as Brendon Frost calls for a target.

(iii) The notice sent to the Chief Constable must contain a description of the shotgun (including any identification number) and the nature of the transaction and the name and address of the other person involved in the transaction. The notice must be sent either by registered post or by recorded delivery.

(d)   When one or both of the parties involved hold a Certificate renewed on or before 30 June 1989 (i.e. an old-style certificate) the following requirements apply:

(i) If both the person transferring and the person acquiring the shotgun have Certificates issued on or before 30 June 1989, neither need comply with any of the new notification requirements.

(ii) If the person transferring the gun holds a Certificate issued or renewed before 30 June 1989, but the person acquiring the gun holds a new-style certificate, the person transferring the gun must enter details of the gun on the new holder's Certificate. The new holder of the gun must send a notice of the transaction to the Chief Constable within seven days.

(iii) If the person acquiring the gun holds an old-style Certificate and the person transferring the gun holds a new-style Certificate, the person transferring the gun should send a notice of the transaction to the Chief Constable, but the person receiving the gun need not notify his Chief Officer of Police.

Targets that are only seen momentarily in trees can be very difficult.

Purchasing of Shotgun Ammunition

Whatever date your Certificate was issued, from 1 July 1989 you must produce your Shotgun Certificate when purchasing shotgun ammunition, unless you are exempt from the need to hold a Certificate. If your gun is classified as a firearm, you will need to produce your Firearm Certificate.

Young Persons

(a)   If you are under fifteen and have a Shotgun Certificate, you may have with you an assembled shotgun provided you are supervised by a person over twenty-one or the shotgun is in a gun cover and securely fastened.

(b)   If you are fifteen or over and have a Shotgun Certificate, you may be given a shotgun as a gift.

Exemptions

You do *not* need a shotgun certificate if:

(a)   you borrow a shotgun from the occupier of private premises (including land) and use it thereon in his presence;

(b)   you use someone else's shotgun on artificial targets at a place and time approved by the local Chief Officer of Police. (Application should be made to the local police who will then issue a written exemption);

(c)   you possess a Northern Ireland Firearms Certificate for a shotgun;

(d)   you are in possession of a weapon (for

which someone else holds a Certificate) in a theatrical or film production;

(e) your weapon is an antique firearm which has been sold, transferred, purchased, acquired or is possessed as a curiosity or ornament;

(f) you are under instruction from another person who holds a Certificate and you are carrying a weapon for his/her use for sporting purposes only;

(g) you are engaged in business as a registered firearms dealer;

(h) you are in possession of a weapon in the course of the business of an auctioneer, carrier, warehouseman or a slaughterer of animals;

(i) you are in possession of a weapon on board a ship, or as a signalling apparatus on board an aircraft or at an aerodrome.

Appeals

If the police refuse to grant, vary or renew a Firearm or Shotgun Certificate in England and Wales you may appeal to the Crown Court giving notice within twenty-one days to the Administrator of the Crown Court and the Chief Officer of Police. In Scotland, you may appeal to the Sheriff Court.

Offences

It is an offence to infringe any of the Act's requirements. There are also specific offences covered by the Firearms Act 1968; which are:

(a) to trade in any way in shotguns without being registered with the police as a dealer;

(b) to shorten the barrel of a shotgun to less than 24 inches;

(c) to convert in any way an imitation into a lethal weapon;

(d) to possess a shotgun or ammunition with intent to injure;

(e) to use a real or imitation shotgun to resist arrest;

(f) to carry a real or imitation shotgun with intent to commit a crime;

(g) to supply a shotgun to anyone who is prohibited from having one;

(h) to carry without lawful authority or reasonable excuse a loaded shotgun or air weapon or any other firearms, whether loaded

Ken Williamson is a well-known Sporting shooter. Here he concentrates fully on his next target.

or not, together with ammunition suitable for use in that firearm;

(i)   to sell, lend or give a shotgun to anyone who has not got a Shotgun Certificate. The penalty for doing so is imprisonment or a fine or both;

(j)   to make a gift of a shotgun to anyone under fifteen years of age. The penalty for doing so is a fine;

(k)   to trespass, without reasonable excuse, with a shotgun in a building or on land;

(l)   to acquire, possess or use any firearm or ammunition for five years after release from any detention or imprisonment of three months or more, but less than three years.

Note: Anyone who has been sentenced to preventative detention or to imprisonment or to corrective training for a term of three years or more shall not at any time have a firearm in their possession;

(m)   the penalty for possession of a firearm without appropriate authority is six months imprisonment or a fine up to £2,000.

Proof

(a)   Proof is the compulsory testing of every shotgun to ensure its safety before it is offered for sale. Reproof is the similar testing of a shotgun which has gone out of proof by reason of alteration or wear.

There is nothing else in this competitor's mind but the target he is about to call for.

(b)   The Gun Barrel Proof Acts 1868, 1950 and 1978 lay down that no shotgun may be sold, exchanged or exported, exposed or kept for sale or exchanged or pawned unless and until it has been fully proved and duly marked with a recognized proof mark.

(c)   The offence of dealing in unproved arms is committed by the seller, not by any unwitting purchaser.

(d)   If you are doubtful about the proof of your firearm, you should take it to a gunmaker or to the London Proof House, 48, Commercial Road, London EL1 1LP, or to the Birmingham Proof House, Banbury Street, Birmingham B5 5RH.

It is also a requirement of the new act that the gun owner is entirely responsible for the security of shotguns outside the home. The CPSA offer the following advice to shooter's carrying weapons to and from events by car and in hotels. When the car is parked temporarily at a restaurant, for example, ensure that:

(a)   guns and ammunition are locked in the boot;

(b)   all shooting clothing is out of sight;

(c)   there are no obvious signs in or on the car that you may be carrying guns, for example, car stickers, badges, magazines, etc;

(d)   if possible, the car is positioned so that it is on view to you during the halt;

(e)   the car itself is locked.

At an hotel, ask the manager to deposit the guns in the hotel strongroom. If the hotel does not possess such a facility, take the guns with you to your hotel room. Split them into their main sections (barrels, fore-end, stock) and lock them in their gun cases, putting the fore-ends in a separate locked suitcase, car boot or friend's room. Always ensure that you lock your hotel room when you leave it.

There is not doubt that some politicians and police officers wish to see private ownership of firearms prohibited completely. It is therefore in the interests of all shooters that people who possess sporting weapons behave with the utmost responsibility at all times. In so doing, they will deny those who oppose shooting the opportunity to find a platform for their vociferous and misleading propaganda.

Appendix II

RULES FOR EACH DISCIPLINE

Reproduced by kind permission of the Clay Pigeon Shooting Association.

English Sporting

1. Targets: FITASC targets (mini, midi, battue, rocket and rabbit) may be used as well as normal ISU targets for skeet and Olympic Trap. The FITASC targets shall not exceed 30 per cent of the total number of targets in the competition.
2. Targets thrown: Targets may be thrown as singles, report pairs, following pairs or simultaneous pairs. Targets will be thrown by silent and non-visible instruction by the referee after the shooter has pronounced the word 'Ready.' The release shall take place at any time up to three seconds after the shooter has pronounced the word 'Ready.'
3. Guns: All shotguns, including semi-automatics, are allowed providing their calibre does not exceed 12 gauge.

Shotguns must not be loaded with more than two cartridges. Straps on guns are forbidden except for handicapped persons who have been given express permission by the organizers.

In the case of a shooter not complying with these regulations, all targets on that particular stand or stands shall be counted as lost.

It is forbidden to use another person's gun without his permission.

4. Cartridges. The load of cartridges shall not exceed 28 grams of shot. The shot shall be spherical shot of normal production lead, diameter between 2 and 2.6mm, English sizes 6–9. Plated shot may be used. Home loads may not be used. The referee may at any time take an unfired cartridge out of a shooter's gun for examination. If the cartridge is found not to comply with the regulations, all targets on that particular stand will be counted as lost.

5. A report pair. This is a pair where the second target is launched at the sound of the gun firing at the first target.
6. A following pair. This is a pair where the second target is launched as soon and as safely as possible after the first target, from the same trap.
7. A simultaneous pair. Is a pair where both targets are launched simultaneously.
8. Trajectories. At each stand, the trajectories shall be the same for each shooter in height, distance and speed. It must be possible for all the targets to be hit within the effective range of a 12-bore shotgun. Before a shoot, organizers will establish a scheme for the trajectories of targets. These trajectories, established and calculated in calm weather, may be altered by wind, but if so altered, will remain regular targets.
9. Targets killed. The target is killed when it has been launched and the shooter has shot it according to the rules and at least one visible bit has broken off, or it has been totally or partially pulverized.
10. A target is missed:
(a) when it has not been hit;
(b) if only dusted or deflected;
(c) if the shooter is unable to fire because he has left the safety catch on, has forgotten to load or cock, the gun has been insufficiently broken or closed or the shooter has forgotten to take the necessary measures to load the chamber (when he uses a single-barrel gun);
(d) if it is the fourth or more malfunction of

the gun, or ammunition, occurring at the same stand;

(e) if the shooter is unable to fire his second shot, having not put in a second cartridge, or if he has not cancelled the locking device of the loading chamber of an automatic weapon, or if the safety catch engages due to recoil of the first shot, or if the second cartridge is ejected by the recoil or opened and emptied by the recoil for any other reason;

(f) if the second shot cannot be fired because a shooter using a single-trigger gun has not released the trigger sufficiently having fired his first shot;

(g) if the shooter, in the case of malfunction, opens it himself or touches the safety catch before the referee has examined the gun;

(h) if the shot is not fired for another reason which does not give right to another target;

(i) if the shooter (without legitimate reason) does not shoot at a regular double;

(j) if the shooter (without legitimate reason) does not shoot the second target of a regular double, the result of the first is scored and the second declared lost.

11. Shooting position. The shooter will position himself within the area of the shooting stand. He is allowed to load his gun only on the stand, his gun always pointing down the range, and only when the referee has given the signal to start shooting.

In no case may a shooter move to the stand before the preceding shooter has left the stand and it is his turn to shoot. Shooting stands shall be clearly defined squares of 0.91m a side.

12. Gun position. Gun position in relation to the shoulder shall be optional when the shooter calls for the target, providing it complies with rule 11 (shooting position).

13. Viewing point. Any shooter who has not had an opportunity to see targets on any stand, i.e. at the commencement of shooting each day, shall have the right to be shown it/them. He must watch these from a position specified by the shoot organizer.

14. Shooting and sighting. Shooting and sighting practice is not allowed. A shooter can only fire on his turn and only when a target has been launched. It is forbidden to aim or shoot other shooters' targets. It is also forbidden to

aim or fire on purpose at living animals/birds. Any such action shall lead to immediate disqualification without the return of entry fee.

15. Roll-call. On roll-call, the shooter must be ready to fire immediately and must take with him sufficient ammunition and equipment for the stand. The referee shall warn the following shooter to be prepared to shoot.

16. Gun malfunctions. The shooter shall be allowed three gun or ammunition malfunctions not attributable to him on each stand without being penalized. The fourth or later malfunction shall be counted as lost or pair lost.

In the case of jamming of the gun, which in the referee's opinion cannot be repaired on the spot without being the shooter's fault, the shooter will be allowed to fire with another gun if he can get one immediately. Otherwise he may shoot his remaining targets later, but only with the referee's permission.

In the case of misfiring or malfunction, the shooter has to remain where he is, the gun pointed down the range, not opened, and without touching the safety catch before the referee has examined the gun.

Two cartridges can be used on each single target, but the shooter will only be allowed two cartridges for each double.

In the case of a gun or ammunition malfunction on a single target, provided the shooter has been able to fire one shot, the result shall be scored.

In the doubles, the shooter has the right to shoot either of the targets first. Should the shooter kill both targets together with either the first or the second shot, then the results will be scored pair killed.

In a double, the shooter, having missed his first target, may fire his second cartridge at the same target.

When shooting a report pair or a following pair, the shooter will have the right if he misses the first target to fire his second cartridge at the same target, the result being scored on the first target, the second target being counted as lost.

17. No Target. The clay will be 'No Target' and a new target will be launched, the shooter having fired or not, if:

(a) the target is broken at the start;

(b) the target is launched from the wrong trap;

(c) two targets are launched simultaneously when a single should have been thrown;

(d) the target is definitely of another colour than the targets used for the competition at that stand;

(e) the first or second target of a double is irregular;

(f) two targets are launched simultaneously during a report pair or a following pair;

(g) the target is launched before the shooter has said 'Ready';

(h) the target is launched after a delay of more than three seconds;

(i) the target zigzags or its initial speed is not sufficient, or its trajectory is irregular;

(j) the shooter misses his first target and this target collides with the second before the shooter has fired his second shot.

In the case of a 'No Target' in any form of doubles, the shooter will be asked to fire a second double to determine the scores of the two shots. This will also apply in the case of malfunction of gun or ammunition not attributable to the shooter, provided that it is not the fourth time on that stand.

The referee may also order the launching of a new target when:

(a) the shooter has been materially disturbed;

(b) another competitor fires at the same target;

(c) the referee cannot decide for any reason if the target has been killed or lost.

The referee cannot in any case give a 'No Target' if the shooter has missed for any reason other than those stated in the 'No Target' rules.

The shooter must not turn round before he has opened his gun and removed the cartridges. In the case of a 'No Target' the gun must be opened and the cartridges removed. It can only be closed when firing resumes.

18. Referee's duties. The referee's decision can be brought to the attention of the jury in writing. If the jury finds the protest valid it can give the referee direction for future decisions or elect a new referee or finally overrule the referee's decision in so far as this does not concern lost or killed targets or irregular targets, where the referee's decision is final.

If the shooter or the team's captain does not agree with the referee about a shot, a complaint must be made immediately the incident occurs, by raising an arm and saying 'Protest.'

The referee must then stop the shooting and give his decision. In no case will it be permitted to pick up a target to see if it has been shot.

The referee under the control of the jury shall see to the application of the rules, keep the onlookers silent and out of the way, and see that the shooters have a clear view from the shooting stand.

If a shooter or team's captain is of the opinion that the score announced is not correct, he must immediately make a complaint to the referee. The referee must then immediately check the result after which he shall make his decision known. If the complainant does not agree with this decision he shall present the jury with a short written notice of the incident.

A referee can, in exceptional circumstances, interrupt the shooting at any time. This interruption may only take place when a shooter has finished shooting and before another one commences.

The referee may be assisted by a marker, particularly in big championships.

The principal function of the marker is to keep a record on a score sheet of the result of each shot as it is called by the referee.

The referee has to decide immediately if a new target is to be launched due to irregularity. He should say 'No Target' before the shooter fires.

19. Jury. At every competition a jury of five shooters representative of the shooters present shall be appointed. A chairman shall be elected who shall have a casting vote in the case of equal voting. The jury can make valid decisions when the chairman and two members are present. In urgent cases, two members of the jury who arrive at a unanimous decision may take such a decision after consultation with the referee of the stand concerned.

Any protest to the jury shall be accompanied by a protest fee which is non-returnable if the protest is lost.

The duties of the jury are to:

(a) verify that, before shooting begins, the stands conform with the regulations, and the arrangements in general are suitable and correct;

Jeremy Welham is one of Britain's finest Sporting shooters. See how his finger is resting lightly on the trigger as he prepares to mount.

Here is a high-driven bird floating into the shooter's sight.

(b)   see during shooting that rules are adhered to and that guns, ammunition and targets are examined by random test;
(c)   make decisions in connection with technical defects or other disturbances in the shooting if these are not resolved by the referee;
(d)   deal with protests;
(e)   make decisions regarding penalties if a competitor does not adhere to the rules or deports himself in an unsportsmanlike manner;
(f)   make sure that at least two members of the jury are always present on the shooting ground.

If the shooter uses guns or ammunition not corresponding to rules, all shots fired with these weapons or ammunition are considered 'Lost'.

If the jury finds that the violation has been done intentionally it can disqualify the shooter. If, however, the jury finds the shooter could not be aware of the violation and has not gained real advantage, it may be decided to accept the result under condition that the fault is corrected and acknowledged.

Other than in rules concerning disqualification, violation of the rules will normally incur first a warning from the referee or a member of the jury. In the case of further or more important offences, the jury may fine the shooter with a lost target or, in more serious cases, disqualify him from the competition.

If a shooter does not present himself after being called three times, he will normally forfeit three targets, taken from the first three killed targets of that stand. The jury may give him the opportunity to shoot his remaining targets later, at a time specified by the referee.

If the jury notices a shooter deliberately delaying the competition or acting in a dishonest, dishonourable or intemperate manner, it may give him a warning or fine him one target or disqualify him from the competition.

When the jury fines the shooter one target and does not specify which one in particular, the first killed target after the verdict must be considered lost. If the shooter has finished the day's shooting, the target is deducted from the last stand on the card.
20.   Ties. Ties for first place will be decided by shooting as follows: a stand will be drawn and the tied shooters will shoot the stand again. If this does not resolve the tie, then it will be shot again, miss and out. All other results for trophies or article prizes will be by shoot off. All divisible prizes by add and divide.
21.   Team ties. Team ties shall be resolved as for individual ties, by shooting the tie between the highest scorers of each team as in the rule on ties (*see* section 20).

All shooters are required to have acquainted themselves with the current regulations which apply to shooting under English Sporting Rules.

By taking part in the competition, they accept the penalties and other consequences resulting from violation of the rules and referee's order. The rules shall be posted in a prominent position.

International Sporting

Shooting Stand

Art. 1 Following the configuration of the ground, a Sporting layout must be equipped with a sufficient amount of traps so that the competitors will shoot under conditions as close as possible to game shooting – partridges, pheasant, ducks, rabbits, infront, low, high, crossing and quartering in battue, in fields or in woods, hidden or not by trees and bushes.

The ground must have been approved by the national federation for the organization of national competitions and by the international federation for the organization of the international competitions.

Clays

Art. 2 The clays to be used are the regular trench, skeet and rabbit-shooting clays, thinner clays and clays with a smaller diameter which have a higher speed, and possibly electric targets.

Shooting Position

Art. 3 The shooter will adopt the standing position, his feet within the limits of the shooting stand, his gun held with two hands clearly out of the shoulder, gun touching the body under the armpit. He will keep this position until the bird or birds are in sight.

The departure of the birds is given by the referee after the shooter has pronounced the word 'Ready' (*'Prêt'*).

If the marksman positions himself wrongly or shoulders his gun before the target appears, he will receive a warning. A second fault will cause a 'No Bird' and, if there is a third fault in the same run (sequence), a 'Nought' ('Zero') will be called, or, in the case of a double, a 'Zero, Zero'.

The shooter has no right to refuse the bird unless he has not pronounced the word 'Ready'.

Shooting posts will be marked by squares of 0.91m on one side or circles of 1m diameter.

When the bird is in sight, the shooter must shoulder his gun in order to fire it at all the clays, even the rabbits.

Trajectories

Art. 4   For the championships or international championships, a Sporting Committee will be formed which will be entrusted with the task of fixing, at the latest the day before the competition, the different trajectories of the clays which will be shot during the event. No training will be permitted before the events take place on the course of courses (*parcours*) fixed by the technical committee.

At each stand, the setting of the trajectories for all the shooters must be strictly the same in height, distance and speed.

Before the championship, the shoot organizer will establish a plan showing the trajectories of the traps. These trajectories, established and calculated in calm weather, may be altered by wind.

Irregular Birds

Art. 5   The following are considered as irregular birds:
(a)   Two birds launched at the same time for a single.
(b)   Birds broken on leaving the trap. Under no circumstances will the result of shooting a 'No-Bird' be counted.
Irregular doubles:

(a)   Either or both birds in a double are irregular.
(b)   Only one bird is launched in a double. After a judge has declared a 'No Bird', firing cannot continue. After a warning, the marksman will receive a Zero penalty.

Organization of Competitions

Art. 6   Shooting will be in squads of a maximum of six shooters. If necessary it is permissible to form squads of at least three shooters.

The organizing committee, in agreement with the jury, can fill vacancies by non-competitive shooters who will shoot for 'birds only'.

Art. 7   During international competitions, the shooters of each country shall be dispersed over the various squads. The organizing committee will announce the arrangements for a draw at a previously determined hour so that national delegates can be present.

If, during the draw for the shooting squads, members of a family find themselves in the same group, they will be able, before the competition begins, to ask the organizing committee to regroup them in different squads of shooters.

Art. 8   Shooting takes place in squads of six shooters as drawn, with moving up of the shooter not only at each stand but also for shooting doubles when certain stands call for the shooting of doubles.

At each stand the six shooters of a squad will first fire at the single birds and, if necessary, the six shooters will then fire at the doubles. For example:
Stand 1.   Singles, shooting in the following order: 1, 2, 3, 4, 5, 6.
Stand 1.   Doubles, in the following order: 2, 3, 4, 5, 6, 1.
Stand 2.   Singles, in the following order: 3, 4, 5, 6, 1, 2.
Stand 2.   Doubles, in the following order: 4, 5, 6, 1, 2, 3.
All the targets will be exhibited once at post 1 and subsequently only new targets will be shown. The shooters are not allowed to fire or swing their guns at the birds.

Art. 9 Shooting occurs in sequences of twenty-five or thirty birds, singles, simultaneous doubles, doubles 'on the gun', in which the second bird is thrown only when a shot has been fired at the first target, and rafale doubles.

However, the referee can, in exceptional circumstances, interrupt shooting if there is sudden heavy rainfall or a storm which seems to be of short duration.

Art. 10 If one of the shooters is not present when his name is called, the referee must call his name and number loudly three times during a period of one minute. If the shooter does not then appear, shooting will start without him.

Once the first bird of this series is shot, a late-arriving shooter can only take his place in the group if the first shooter of the group has not yet taken up his position to shoot his second bird.

During a championship, any shooter who does not answer when his name is called will be allowed to shoot in another squad but his first three killed birds will be scored zero.

Art. 11 In the case of a malfunction of a trap during the shoot, the referee will decide if the round must be continued on another stand or on the same one after the mechanical trouble has been rectified. The squad has the right to see another bird before starting again.

Art. 12 During international competitions, the scores will be kept by three persons.

Immediately after each series, the scores are compared and the possible differences are resolved for each bird. The scores of each series are then posted on a central notice-board.

Art. 13 On the course (*parcours*) chosen by the technical committee (*see* Art. 19(a)) it will not be possible to shoot targets in training.

Referees and Jury

Art. 14 Shooting will be supervised by a referee who normally has to be in possession of a referee's certificate and has clay shooting experience. His principal role consists of deciding, after each bird is thrown, whether the bird is killed or not and clearly signifying if it has been lost or irregular.

Art. 15 The referee will be assisted by two auxiliaries and a marker whom he will have chosen from the preceding squad. Shooters are not allowed to refuse to do this job, but the referee can accept a substitute.

The principal function of the auxiliary referees is to record on a score sheet the results which they ascertain. The marker has to record on a score sheet the results announced by the referee.

Art. 16 The referee has to decide immediately if a new bird must be launched following a technical difficulty or for any other reason. He has to say 'No Bird', if possible, before the shooter fires his first shot.

Art. 17 The principal referee takes all the decisions alone. If one of the auxiliary referees holds another opinion, he should raise his arm to inform the principal referee who will then make a definitive decision.

Jury

Art. 18 International events will be supervised by a jury consisting of a representative of each country participating, with the representative of the organizing country as chairman.

The jury makes decisions by a majority vote. In the case of equal votes, the chairman's vote is final. The jury can make valid decisions when the chairman and two members are present.

In urgent cases, two members who are unanimous over a decision can, by way of exception, make it in consultation with the referee.

Art. 19 The role of the jury is:

(a) to appoint a technical committee in order to fix, on the day before the competition, the various trajectories, the location of the shooting stands, the choice and speed of the targets which will be shot during the event;

(b) to verify before shooting begins that the range conforms to regulations and that the preparatory arrangements are suitable and correct;

(c) to see that during shooting, the rules are adhered to and to inspect the weapons, ammunition and targets by means of test or otherwise;

(d) to make the necessary decisions in cases of technical defects or other disturbances during shooting if these are not resolved by the referee;

(e) to deal with protests;

(f) to make decisions regarding penalties when it concerns a shooter who does not adhere to the rules or behaves in an unsportsmanlike manner;

(g) to make sure that there are always at least two members of the jury present at the shooting ground;

Art. 20 The decisions of the jury cannot be appealed against unless a special appeal jury has been appointed for the competition.

Art. 21 Weapons and Ammunition. All weapons, including automatics, are allowed provided their calibre does not exceed 12-bore. No handicap will be given to shooters using guns of a calibre smaller than 12.

Any changing of weapon (or any part of the weapon which functions normally, adjustable chokes included) is forbidden throughout the duration of the competition.

Any infringement of this rule will automatically lead to the disqualification of the competitor.

Art. 22 The load of the cartridge may not exceed 36 grams of shot. The shot will be spherical and of solid lead, diameter between 2 and 2.5mm.

Cartridges must be normally loaded. The use of dispersers or dispersion devices or abnormal loading of cartridges is forbidden (including reversed loading).

The referee can, at any moment, take an unfired cartridge out of the shooter's gun for examination. The use of black powder is forbidden as well as the use of tracer cartridges.

Art. 23 In case of jamming of the gun which, on the referee's decision, cannot be repaired on the spot, without being the shooter's fault, the latter will be allowed to fire with another gun if he can get one immediately.

Otherwise he will have to leave his place and round and will shoot his remaining birds in another round where there is room with the referee's permission. If the gun is repaired before the round is finished by his squad, the shooter can take his place on the squad again, with the referee's permission.

In case of another malfunction of the gun or the cartridges, resulting in inability to fire, and without it being the shooter's fault, the latter may choose to change guns or continue with the same.

He will have the right to another bird three times during the same round of twenty-five birds in all the cases of malfunction described in the rules without taking into consideration whether he has changed his gun or not.

The fourth malfunction and the following will be scored as 'Zero'.

Art. 24 Two cartridges can be used on each single bird, but the shooter will only be allowed two cartridges for each double.

In the doubles, the shooter has the right to shoot either of the two birds first.

In a double, if the two birds are killed with one shot, they will be scored 'Killed – Killed'. If the shooter misses the first bird, he may fire his second cartridge at the same bird.

When shooting a double 'on the gun', the shooter will have the right, if he misses the first bird, to fire his second shot at the same bird, the result being counted on the first bird, the second bird being counted 'Zero'.

Art. 25 When a shooter is ready to fire, he announces 'Ready' to the trapper and the bird must be launched within the time of 0 to 3 seconds.

When the shooter has announced 'Ready', he has to stick to the position described in Art. 3. until the bird is in sight.

Killed or Missed Birds

Art. 26 The bird is killed when it has been launched and the shooter has shot it according to the rules and at least one visible bit of it has broken off or it has been totally or partly pulverized.

Art. 27 The bird is missed:

(a) when it has not been hit;

(b) if only dust goes off (smoked or deflected bird);

(c) if the shooter is unable to fire because he left the safety catch on, has forgotten to load or cock, if the gun has not been sufficiently broken or closed or if the shooter has forgotten to take the necessary measures to load the cartridge chamber (when he uses a single-barrel gun);

(d) if it is the fourth or more malfunction of the gun or ammunition occurring in the same round of twenty-five birds;

(e) if the shooter is unable to fire his second shot because he has not put in a second cartridge or if he has not cancelled the locking device of the loading chamber in an automatic weapon, or if the safety catch engages due to the recoil of the first shot or if the second cartridge is ejected by the recoil or opened and emptied due to the recoil or for any other reason;

(f) if the second shot cannot be fired because a shooter using a single-trigger gun has not released it sufficiently after having fired his first shot;

(g) if the shooter, in case of malfunction, opens it himself or touches the safety catch before the referee has examined the gun;

(h) if the shot is not fired for another reason which does not give right to another bird;

(i) if the shooter adopts a waiting position which is not according to Art. 3. and if he has been warned once during the same round.

New Clay – 'No Bird'.

Art. 28   The clay will be 'No Bird' and a new target will be launched, the shooter having fired or not if:

(a) the bird is broken at the start;

(b) the bird is launched from the wrong trap;

(c) two birds are launched simultaneously when a single should have been thrown;

(d) the bird is definitely of another colour than the birds used for the competition;

(e) the first bird of a double is regular and the second irregular, or conversely;

(f) two birds are launched simultaneously during a double 'on the gun'.

Art. 29   The bird will be declared 'No Bird' and a new bird will be launched, the shooter *not* having fired if:

(a) the bird is launched before the shooter has said 'Ready';

(b) the bird is launched after a delay of more than 3 seconds;

(c) the bird zigzags, if its initial speed is not sufficient or its trajectory is irregular;

(d) the shooter is not in the waiting or shooting position prescribed by the rules (first warning).

No complaint of irregularity will be accepted when, in singles as well as doubles, the bird or birds have been shot at, if the irregularity in question consists simple of either a normal deviation of the trajectory of the bird or of a premature or delayed release, unless the referee has distinctly called 'No Bird' before the shooter has fired in the case of a premature release, or before the appearance of the bird in the case of a delayed release. In all other cases, the result will be counted when a shooter has fired.

Art. 30   In case of misfiring of the cartridge or a malfunction of the gun not attributable to the shooter, the bird will be declared 'No Bird' and a new bird will be launched; but after three misfires or malfunctions in the same round of twenty-five birds (the shooter having exchanged guns or not) further incidents will be scored as lost.

Art. 31   The referee may also order the launching of a new bird when:

(a) the shooter has been clearly disturbed;

(b) another competitor fires at the same target;

(c) the referee for any reason cannot decide if the bird has been killed or lost. The referee must also consult his assistants before allowing a new bird under this rule.

The referee cannot in any case give a 'No Bird' if the shooter has missed for any other reason than the ones stated in the 'No Bird' rules.

Art. 32   The rules of Art. 23 to Art. 28 apply equally to the firing of doubles, simultaneous doubles and rafale doubles and will be interpreted as follows:

(a) The double will be declared 'No Bird' and the shooter will be asked to fire a second double to determine the scores of the two shots if:

(i) the first bird is regular and the second irregular without taking into account whether the first one is killed or not;

(ii) a malfunction of the gun or cartridge prevents the shooter from shooting his first bird;

(iii) one or the other bird from a double is irregular and the shooter does not fire. If the irregularity in question is a deviation from the normal trajectory, an insufficient speed or a too quick or to slow launching and the two birds have been shot at, the results must be counted;

(iv) the first bird is regular and has been shot at but the second bird is late or does not leave the trap.

If the shooter misses his first bird and this collides with the second before the shooter has fired his second shot; if the fragments of the first bird break the second before the shooter has fired his second shot;

(v) the referee denies the right of the shooter to fire his second shot because of the violation of Art. 3, provided that the shooter has not been warned for the same reason during the same round; otherwise the result of the first shot will be scored and the second bird declared 'Lost';

(vi) in a double, the first bird is missed and the second shot cannot be fired because of malfunction of the gun or ammunition.

(b) The bird will be declared 'Lost':

(i) on the fourth malfunction of the gun or misfiring of the cartridge in the same round;

(ii) if the shooter (without legitimate reason) does not shoot a regular double;

(iii) if the shooter (without legitimate reason) does not shoot the second bird of a regular double. The result of the first bird is scored and the second will be declared 'Lost'.

Art. 33   If during a double the gun fires both shots simultaneously, the double will be declared 'No Bird' and be shot again, even if the first bird has been killed.

Art. 34   A shot will be considered as not fired if:

(a)   the shooter fires although it is not his turn to fire;

(b)   the shooter involuntarily fires a shot on his turn, but before having given the signal.

Art. 35   When shooting doubles 'on the gun' the following will be awarded:

(a)   'Kill' and 'Zero' if the shooter breaks the first bird and misses the second.

(b)   'Kill' and 'No Bird', the double having to be shot again if:

(i) the shooter breaks the first bird and the second bird is irregular;

(ii) the shooter breaks the first bird and a malfunction of his gun or misfire prevents him shooting at his second bird;

(iii) the shooter breaks the first bird but the second bird leaves late or not at all;

(iv) the shooter breaks the first bird but the referee prevents the shooter from firing his second shot owing to the violation of Art. 3.

Providing the shooter has not already been warned for the same reason during the same round, otherwise the result of the first shot will be recorded and the second bird declared 'Lost'.

(c) 'Zero' and 'No Bird', the double having, however, to be shot again if the shooter misses the first bird and the second bird is irregular for one of the reasons given under (b).

The regulations for Art. 24 to 29, 33 and 34, together with the regulations given under point (b); of Art. 32 are applicable to the shooting of doubles 'on the gun'. The last sentence does not apply to Art. 32.

Ground Regulations

Art. 36   All weapons, even unloaded, must be handled with the greatest care. The guns must be carried open; automatic guns must be carried with the breech open and the muzzle pointing upwards and downwards. Straps on guns are forbidden.

When the shooter is not using his gun it must be put vertically in a gun rack or in a similar place. It is forbidden to handle another shooter's gun without his permission.

It is forbidden, during a competition or official championship, for two shooters to fire the same gun. In exceptional cases, owing to malfunctioning of his gun, it is permitted for the shooter to borrow, only during the round in which the incident occurs, the gun of another shooter.

Art. 37   A shooter may only fire on his turn and only when a bird has been thrown. It is forbidden to aim or shoot at other shooter's targets. It is also forbidden to aim or shoot intentionally at living animals or birds.

No pretence of shooting is permitted on the shooting stand.

If a shooter makes, on the shooting stand before saying 'Ready', a pretence of shooting, a referee is obliged to issue a warning to the shooter. After this warning, any similar incident will lead to a zero score for the first target of the series that has been counted as successful.

Art. 38   On roll-call, the shooter must be ready to fire immediately and must take with him sufficient ammunition and equipment for the round.

Art. 39   In no case must a shooter move to the stand before the preceding shooter has left it and it is his turn to shoot.

Art. 40   The shooter is allowed to load his gun only when on the stand of the range where he has taken his place, his gun always pointing down the range and only when the referee has given the sign to start shooting.

Automatic guns must only be loaded with two cartridges.

Art. 41   If the bird or birds of a double are not launched within the three seconds limit, the shooter has to signify that he does not want to shoot it or them by raising his gun in the air and not staying in the waiting position.

Art. 42   The shooter must not turn around before he has broken his gun.

In case of a 'No Bird' or if the shooting is interrupted, the gun must be opened. It can only be closed when firing resumes.

Art. 43   In case of misfiring or malfunctioning of the gun or ammunition, the shooter has to remain where he is, the gun pointed down the range, not broken, and without touching the safety catch before the referee has examined the gun.

Art. 44   The shooting must occur without interruption, the shooter being only allowed to pronounce the necessary words of command to announce 'Ready' or possibly to protest and to answer the referee's questions.

Art. 45   The referee and his auxiliaries, under the control of the jury, see to the application of the rules, keep the onlookers out of the way and see that the shooters have a clear view from all the shooting stands.

Art. 46   If the shooter or the team's captain does not agree with the referee about a shot, the complaint must be made immediately the incident occurs by raising the arm and saying 'Protest' or 'Appeal'.

The referee must then stop the shooting and after consulting his auxiliaries, give his decision. In no case will it be permissible to pick up a bird to see if it has been hit.

Art. 47   The referee's decision may be brought up before the jury, either verbally or in writing.

If the jury finds the protest justified, they can give instructions to the referee for future judgements or elect a new refereee or finally overrule the referee's decision. In no case must this decision concern knowing if a bird is killed or lost or knowing if the bird launched is defective, where no appeal can be made against the referee's decision.

Art. 48   If a shooter or team's captain is of the opinion that the score announced at the end of the series is not correct, he must immediately make a complaint to the referee. The referee must then immediately and in the presence of the scorers, check the result after which he makes his decision known. If the complainant does not agree with the decision, he has to present the jury with a short written protest.

Art. 49   If a shooter or a team's captain or an official sees anything which is not according to the rules, he must advise the referee or a member of the jury.

If the referee cannot take immediate measures, he can refer the reporter to a member of the jury. Referee's decisions can be appealed against by means of a short written notice ot a member of the jury.

Penalties, etc

Art. 50   All shooters are supposed to have acquainted themselves with the current regulations which apply to shooting under *parcours de chasse* rules.

By taking part in the competition, they accept the penalties and other consequences resulting from violation of the rules and referee's orders.

Art. 51   If the shooter uses guns or ammunition not corresponding to the statements of Art. 21 and 22, all shots fired with these weapons or ammunition are considered lost. If the jury finds that the violation had been done intentionally, it can disqualify the shooter. If, however, the jury finds the shooter could not be aware of the violation and has not gained a real advantage, it may decide to accept the result under condition that the fault is corrected and acknowledged.

Art. 52   Violation of the rules first incurs a warning from the referee or a member of the jury. In cases of further or more important

This shooter will not be caught out by a fast bird being driven towards him. The gun is almost in his shoulder already.

offences the jury may fine the shooter with a lost bird or in more serious cases disqualify him from the round or even the competition.

Art. 53   If a shooter does not present himself in his turn after being called three times, he will forfeit three birds taken from the first three killed birds of his following round. The jury may give him the opportunity to shoot his remaining birds later, at a time specified by the referee.

The shooter who refuses to act as auxiliary referee when this is required of him or obviously delays in taking up his position, will be penalized with the loss of a bird.

Art. 54   If the jury notices a shooter deliberately delaying the competition or acting in a dishonest and dishonourable manner, it may give him a warning or fine him one bird or disqualify him from the competition.

Art. 55   When the jury fines a shooter one bird and does not specify which in particular, the first killed bird after the verdict must be considered as lost.

If the shooter has finished the day's shooting, the bird is deducted from the last round.

Tie Shooting

Art. 56   If two or more shooters score the same results in a championship, the shoot off for the first three places will occur on new rounds of twenty-five birds until a difference shows up.

Shooting goes on according to the rules although squads need not consist of six shooters. If no time has been announced for the tie shoot, those shooters concerned must remain in contact with the organizers in order to be able to start shooting not less than half an hour after the end of the ordinary competition.

Art. 57   For the fourth and subsequent places, precedence is decided by the scores in the last round.

Should this still result in a tie, the next to last round is considered, and so on. Finally, a decision may be reached by drawing lots.

Art. 58   If two or more teams have the same score, and if no special rules have been put in the programme, the shooting will be held under the terms of Art. 56 between the teams to find the winners. With regard to the other places, the shooting will be held in accordance with the terms of Art. 57.

Down the Line

Procedure

The trap and targets are set out, targets being in groups of twenty-five in stages, according to the numbers set out (*see* 3, below). The five shooters in the squad shoot in turn (Down the Line) at single targets released at permitted varying angles, on command.

1.   Shooting order. The shooters comprising the squad shall stand at the designated firing marks from one to five (from left to right facing the trap) in the order in which their names appear on the score card. All guns shall be open and empty.

2.   Shooting Down the Line

(a)   When all is ready and correct the referee shall call 'Line Ready'.

(b)   All competitors may then load with two cartridges.

(c)   The first competitor only shall adopt a shooting stance and call 'Pull' or some other word of command.

(d)   Whereupon, the puller (unless acoustic release is in use), who shall be behind the line of shooters, shall immediately release a target.

(e)   The first shooter may shoot at this target in flight with one or two shots. The resulting score is recorded.

If the competitor scores a 'Kill' with the first shot the competitor shall be awarded three points. If the competitor scores a 'Kill' with the second shot he shall be awarded two points. If the competitors fails to kill the target with either shot, the target shall be called 'lost' and no points shall be awarded.

(f)   Provided that a 'No Bird' has not been called and the referee has announced the result of the shot, the shooter on the second firing mark may then follow the same procedure, followed afterwards by the third shooter and repeated for the fourth and fifth.

(g) After Shooter No. 5 has shot, Shooter 1 shall again call for a target and this sequence is followed by all the shooters in the squad until the required number of targets have been shot at.

Each competitor shall shoot at each firing mark:

(i) In a 10-bird stage: two targets.
(ii) In a 15-bird stage: three targets.
(iii) In a 20-bird stage: four targets.
(iv) In a 25-bird stage: five targets.

At such point, an audible signal shall be given and the refereee shall call 'Change'.

Each shooter (except No. 5) then moves to the firing mark next on the right and No. 5 takes the place of No. 1.

When walking between firing marks, each shooter must ensure that the gun is open.

The shooter leaving No. 5 firing mark to take up position at No. 1 firing mark must move to that position by walking behind the line of shooters with gun open and empty of cartridges or cases.

When all is in order and all the shooters are again in proper position, the referee shall call 'Line Ready' and shall do so after each change and before the commencement of shooting.

The No. 1 of the squad (after the first move and standing at No. 2 firing mark) commences the second round, at the end of which the squad again moves to the right. Shooter 1 also commences the third and remaining rounds, finishing at the No. 5 firing mark.

When all the members of the squad have shot at the required number of targets from each firing mark, this will conclude the shooting of this particular stage. At this point the referee shall call 'Unload and check your scores' whereupon all the guns shall be opened and emptied of cartridges or cases.

3. The number of stages in a competition is as follows:

(a) For a 50-bird competition: two stages of twenty-five targets.
(b) For a 75-bird competiton: three stages of twenty-five targets.
(c) For a 100-bird competition: four stages of twenty-five targets.

For competitions of less than fifty birds, the organizing committee may use their discretion to decide on the number of stages to be shot so long as the equity of the competition is maintained.

4. Ammunition.

(a) Cartridge specification: maximum bore, 12 gauge. Maximum size of shot: 2.6mm diameter (No. 6 English) and spherical. Maximum load: 28 grams. The shot pellets may be plated.

(b) Home loaded, black powder, incendiary or tracer cartridges are not permitted at registered events or other designated championships and can be prohibited by the club or ground organizing any other type of event is so desired.

(c) Not more than two cartridges may be placed in any part of a gun at any one time.

(d) The referee or jury may inspect a competitor's cartridges at any time without giving a reason.

5. Balk: This is any occurrence which in the opinion of the referee materially handicaps the competitor after the call of 'Pull', if it deters the competitor from shooting or distracts at the moment of shooting.

(a) After the balk, the referee shall declare a 'No Bird'.

(b) Only the competitor directly concerned may claim a balk.

(c) Any claims must be made immediately after the incident in question. Later claims, however presented, will not be permitted.

(d) A claim for a balk which is upheld also constitutes a 'No Bird' and will entitle the competitor to a repeat target.

(e) A claim for a balk which is not upheld will be scored accordingly.

6. Competition. Wherever the word competition is used in the following rules, it refers to a single event on a programme, to an entire one-day programme, or to the programme for any one tournament, and must always be so construed by those in charge of such competition.

7. Competitor. A competitor:

(a) shall observe the rules as herein described and any others that may apply especially for the event;

(b) shall shoot and behave in a safe manner at all times;

(c) may load only when permitted by the referee;

(d) is allowed only fifteen seconds to call for a target after the result of the preceding shooter's target has been announced by the referee (or, if No. 1 in the squad, after the referee's call of 'Line Ready'.);

(e) shall remove any cartridge case or unfired cartridge from the gun before turning from the firing mark at the cessation of shooting;

(f) shall be at the firing mark within three minutes of being duly notified;

(g) shall take sufficient cartridges to complete the stage;

(h) shall shoot only from the proper firing mark at the designated clay targets in flight;

(i) shall not shoot at or 'sight' any birds, beasts, other objects or other competitor's clay's;

(j) shall remain at the final firing mark until all the competitors in the squad have completed the stage.

8. Disqualification. Disqualification entails the forfeiture of all entrance money and rights in the competition to which it relates.

9. Duly notified. A competitor is 'duly notified' to compete when his or her name is called out by a referee, scorer or other person authorized to do so.

To assist in notifying competitors, it is strongly recommended that a visible squad marker-board be used and kept up to date.

(a) If a 'squad hustler' is provided it is a matter of courtesy only and does not relieve the competitor of responsibility. It is the duty of each competitor to be ready to compete promptly when called upon to do so.

(b) A competitor shall arrive at the proper firing mark and be ready to shoot within three minutes of being duly notified.

(c) If a competitor is absent after this time, the name on the card shall be called loudly twice in the space of thirty seconds by the referee.

If the shooter is still not present fifteen seconds after this, the referee shall announce 'Absent' and shall without further delay call 'Line Ready' and shooting shall then commence.

(d) In order to participate in a stage, a competitor must be at the proper firing mark at the time the referee calls 'Line Ready'.

No competitor shall be permitted to shoot the stage if arriving after this.

The competitor may be permitted to shoot the missed stage at a later time to be determined by the ground organization in consultation with the jury.

10. Firing mark. A firing mark is:

(a) A clearly designated, reasonably flat area measuring 91cm × 91cm, the front centre of which is 14.6m (16 yards) from the centre of the pivot point of the trap when set to throw a straight-away target.

(b) The distance between the front edge centres of adjacent firing marks shall be 2.74m.

(c) The area from which the competitor shall shoot. The competitor must have both feet entirely within this area when calling for the target and until the completion of the shot (or shots) at that target.

11. Guns. A smooth-bore gun, having a barrel not less than 24 inches in length, not being an air gun.

(a) Shotguns used in competitions or events organized by the CPSA or grounds affiliated to the CPSA must conform to the pertinent Firearms Act.

(b) Within these limitations approved types of shotguns may be used. The calibre shall not exceed 12 bore.

(c) Barrels with attached ventilated recoil eliminators are prohibited.

(d) Semi-automatic shotguns shall be so adjusted that their operation does not inconvenience other competitors.

(e) A shotgun that has malfunctioned twice in any stage of the competition should not be used unless it has been satisfactorily repaired. A competitor having a third or subsequent malfunction in any one stage must abide by the result.

(f) A properly functioning shotgun may not be exchanged for another in the course of a stage unless the referee gives permission.

12. Gun position. The gun may be held in any safe position but it is usual to adopt the 'gun up' position. That is, with the gun butt into the shoulder, loaded, safety catch off, the barrels pointed towards the target flight area and ready to call.

13. Jury. A jury of at least five competent

persons may be appointed for registered events.

(a) The jury should consist where possible of one member of the ground management, one referee, one member of the executive (regional or country committee where possible) and the remainder of the jury of knowledgeable and competent shooters who are listed in the current CPSA averages for DTL.

(b) The jury is responsible for:

(i) approving target flights, angles and distances according to the current rules and prevailing conditions;

(ii) awarding penalties;

(iii) arbitrating on complaints or protests lodged;

(iv) deciding on the competence or otherwise of the referees and scorers and may remove or replace any of these at any time during the competiton;

(v) deciding on the intended meaning of these rules when there is a requirement for interpretation.

(c) The jury may not overrule a referee as to whether a target is hit or not.

14. Killed target: a regular target that in the opinion of the referee has at least a visible piece broken from it, or is completely reduced to dust, or has a visible piece broken from it which is reduced to dust by the competitors' shot.

(a) A target which has some dust removed from it by the shot but otherwise remains intact is not a killed target.

(b) Shot marks on a target in a pick-up are not evidence of a killed target and will not be considered as such.

15. Killed target: a regular target that is not a killed target after having been fired upon in accordance with these rules.

A target shall be declared 'Lost' when:

(a) the target remains unbroken after being fired at;

(b) the competitor, after an apparent malfunction or misfire, opens the gun or moves the safety catch before handing the gun to the referee;

(c) a competitor suffers a third or subsequent malfunction or misfire in the same stage (*See* sections 17 and 18);

(d) an irregular whole target is shot at and missed (unless the referee has called 'No Bird'

before or has done so as the shooter fires his first shot);

(e) The competitor fails to fire for any reason due to personal fault or negligence.

16. Magazine gun: A single-barrelled shotgun capable of holding more than one cartridge at any one time.

17. Malfunction (*See also* Misfire, section 18). The referee shall announce a malfunction and declare a 'No Bird' where there is a failure of a shotgun to fire the cartridge due to some defect of the shotgun mechanism.

(a) An ammunition defect is not a malfunction. Any cause due to the shooter's fault is not a malfunction. 'Jarring back' of the safety catch on the report of the first shot is not a malfunction and the target shall be scored accordingly.

(b) The shooter is allowed a total of two malfunctions in any one stage. Thereafter the result shall be scored.

(c) Second-barrel malfunction. An allowable malfunction on the second shot shall be resolved by the target being declared a 'No Bird'. The competitor shall repeat the target and the result of the second shot only shall be scored.

After calling for the target and its appearance the shooter must fire off the first barrel before firing the second barrel at the target. If the target is killed by the first barrel shot the target will be declared lost.

(d) General safety. Any shotgun which has a malfunction that can cause the shotgun to become unsafe in any way (simultaneous discharge, faulty trigger, breech lock insecure, etc.) shall be declared unsafe by the referee and shall not be used further in the event until properly repaired.

(e) Procedure in the event of a malfunction. The competitor shall, without turning from the firing mark, touching the safety catch, opening the gun or interfering with its mechanism in any way, hand the gun safely to the referee for the referee to inspect and give a decision.

Should the shooter fail in any of these respects the target shall be declared lost.

18. Misfire: failure of the cartridge to fire or function properly after the firing pin has made proper contact with the cartridge cap.

(a) The referee shall announce a misfire and

declare a 'No Bird' when the firing pin indentation is clearly noticeable and:

   (i) the primer only fires;

   (ii) the powder charge is missing;

   (iii) the powder charge does not ignite;

   (iv) the components of the load remain in the barrel.

(b) A shooter is allowed a total of two misfires in any one stage. Thereafter the result shall be scored.

(c) Second-barrel misfires. An allowable misfire on the second shot shall be resolved by the target being declared a 'No Bird'. The competitor shall then repeat the target and the result of the second shot only shall be scored.

After calling for the target and its appearance the shooter must fire the first barrel, before firing the second barrel at the target. If the target is killed by the first barrel shot, the target will be declared lost.

19. 'No Bird'. After a target has been declared a 'No Bird', it is no longer part of the competition and no record of any hits or misses at any 'No Bird' is recorded or of any account.

The referee shall declare a 'No Bird' and another target shall be allowed only if:

(a) the competitor shoots out of turn;

(b) more than one person shoots at the same target;

(c) a shooter shoots from the wrong firing mark;

(d) a broken target is thrown (whether shot at or not);

(e) more than one target is thrown in single rise shooting;

(f) an allowable simultaneous discharge occurs (*see* section 30);

(g) a clay target of an entirely different colour to those used elsewhere in the competition is suddenly thrown and the shooter has not fired;

(h) an irregular whole target appears and is not shot at.

(i) in the opinion of the referee, some occurrence takes place which may materially affect the equity of the competition;

(j) there is a permissible misfire or malfunction.

Claims for a 'No Bird'. When a referee does not declare a 'No Bird' and the competitor in question considers that an award of 'No Bird' should be given, the competitor must consult with the referee immediately after the shot or target in question. If this is not done, no subsequent claims will be entertained.

If after this the shooter is still not satisfied with the referee's decision, a mark shall be made on the score-sheet at the appropriate point for possible later consideration by the jury.

20. Official score. This is the score, having been properly recorded by a person or persons authorized to do so, finally agreed and posted on the main score-board.

21. Penalties. Penalties shall be imposed by the jury or, where there is no jury, by the organizing committee and shall apply for all purposes. They may take the form of a warning, loss of points or disqualification or, in serious cases, the matter may be referred to the CPSA for possible disciplinary action.

(a) A warning will be given by the referee for initial minor transgressions in safety and behaviour.

(b) The referee shall give a warning which shall be recorded on the score-card for a competitor's:

   (i) first foot fault in any one stage;

   (ii) first or second misfire or malfunction in any one stage;

   (iii) delayed call – first interval exceeding fifteen seconds before calling in any one stage.

(c) One point shall be deducted from a competitor's score for:

   (i) the second and each subsequent foot fault in any one stage;

   (ii) each interruption in the sequence of shooting due to insufficient cartridges having been brought to the firing mark;

   (iii) the second and each subsequent interval in excess of fifteen seconds before calling in any one stage.

(d) Three points shall be deducted from a competitor's score for:

   (i) not being present without sufficient cause at the required place and time after being duly notified;

   (ii) any other misdemeanour that shall be deemed not to be in keeping with the spirit of these rules.

Disqualification: Disqualification entails the forfeiture of all entrance money and rights in the competition to which it relates.

A competitor *may* be disqualified for:

(a) serious breaches of safety;

(b) shooting on the grounds from any place other than the firing marks;

(c) shouldering a closed gun other than when on the designated firing mark;

(d) any other valid reason that shall be deemed necessary for the good of the competition in particular and clay-pigeon shooting in general.

A competitor *shall* be disqualified for:

(a) being disorderly;

(b) being intoxicated;

(c) shooting at any live bird or beast or at any objects other than the clay targets in flight.

22. Practice shooting at registered events. Practice targets shall be of the same make and colour as those used in the competition.

(a) One practice regular target shall be made available to be shot at by each member of the squad immediately prior to each stage of a registered competition.

(b) Such targets shall be shot at from the firing marks allotted to each member of the squad in the order shown on the score-card.

(c) Other than (a), no practice shooting shall take place on any layout to be used in the competition.

23. Protests. Protests may be made only by a competitor, the team captain or the team manager.

(a) Unless other rules are displayed, a protest shall be submitted in writing together with a fee not exceeding £10 which shall be returned only if the protest is upheld.

(b) A protest concerning a score or scores must be made immediately after the squad affected has finished shooting.

(c) A protest concerning whether:

(i) the target was hit or not or by which shot;

(ii) the shooter was balked;

(iii) the target was an alleged 'No Bird';

(iv) the target was of widely different colour

must be made immediately after the target or shot in question to the referee in the first instance. If the competitor is still not satisfied, he may take the protest to a jury for consideration.

(d) No protest will be entertained after all the final results have been posted, except for queries regarding the addition of scores.

24. Puller: an authorized person who shall release targets, either electrically or mechanically, immediately after the shooter's call. The puller shall:

(a) have an unobstructed view of the competitors on their firing marks;

(b) have an unobstructed view of the targets in flight;

(c) give an opinion as to whether a target was hit or not when asked by the referee.

25. Referee: a person authorized and competent to adjudicate a stage of a competition in accordance with these rules. Wherever possible, qualified referees should be used.

(a) A referee's decision as to whether a target is killed or not is final.

(b) The referee:

(i) shall consult the scorer and puller only and then announce the final decision where there is some doubt as to the result of any shot;

(ii) shall announce the result of shooting at each target distinctly and loudly by calling 'one' for a first-barrel kill, 'two' for a second-barrel kill, 'Lost' when the target remains unbroken or 'No Bird' as necessary;

(iii) shall adjudicate the competition fairly and according to the current rules;

(iv) shall ensure – and demonstrate if necessary – at the start of a stage, after a breakdown or complaint, that targets are thrown according to the rules;

(v) shall ensure that competitors shoot according to the rules;

(vi) shall have an uninterrupted view of competitors and the clay targets in flight;

(vii) is empowered to challenge the ammunition of any competitor at any time by removing a cartridge for inspection;

(viii) may call upon a jury at any time to arbitrate if so wished. The referee *must* call upon the jury if three or more competitors in the same squad so request, except where the dispute has regard solely to whether a target is killed or not;

(ix) must in the case of an irregular target call 'No Bird' as or before the shooter fires the

Kerry Dinenage, one of Great Britain's best ZZ target shooters.

first barrel, otherwise if the shooter fires the result shall stand.

26. Registered targets. All clay targets shot at from the standard 16-yard mark in certain specified open and approved tournaments are known as registered targets.

(a) Only clubs or grounds affiliated to the CPSA may hold registered events.

(b) The CPSA require an initial inspection of all layouts before authorizing their use for registered events.

(c) The score made at such targets form the basis of the averages for members for the current classification system.

(d) Where a competitor withdraws or is unable, for any reason, to complete the full programme as specified, the score attained at the last completed stage for that competitor should be returned for registration purposes.

(e) Targets shot at in practice or ties connected with any DTL competition are not regarded as registered targets.

27. Regular and irregular targets.

(a) Regular targets. A whole clay target thrown immediately after the shooter's call and in accordance with these rules.

(b) Irregular targets. A whole clay thrown outside the prescribed limits or one thrown before a shooter's call (fast pull) or a material interval of time after a shooter's call (slow pull).

28. Scoring and scorer.

(a) Competitions (unless otherwise stated) shall be scored using the points system:

   (i) Three points for a first-barrel kill.

   (ii) Two points for a second-barrel kill.

   (iii) Zero points for a target not hit by either shot.

(b) The scorer shall:

   (i) keep an accurate record of the result of shots at each target;

   (ii) mark the score-card '1' for kill 1, '2' for kill 2 and '0' for a lost target, as the referee so calls;

   (iii) give an opinion as to whether a target is hit or not, only when asked by the referee;

   (iv) mark the score-card as appropriate to record misfires, malfunctions, foot-faults, safety warnings or interruptions as the referee so directs;

   (v) total the number of kills and points accurately at the completion of the required number of targets;

   (vi) announce the final scores aloud to the referee and assembled squad;

   (vii) sign and ask the referee to countersign the score-card when the scores are finalized.

Note: Each member of the squad is entitled to inspect the completed score-card before it is taken for posting to the main score-board.

29. Setting the traps.

Datum (or reference point).

(a) All measurements are taken with reference to the top surface of firing mark 3 (the datum point).

(b) Allowances must be made where the ground is at a different level to this datum.

(c) Distances, where given, are all measured from the centre of the pivot point of the trap when it is set to throw a straight-away target.

(d) Care should be taken that traps are set in still weather. Slight adjustments may be necessary in certain wind conditions.

Target height. At a distance of 10 yards from the trap, a regular target shall attain a height of 8 to 10 feet. To ensure the correct elevation, procure an 8-foot pole with a hoop 2 feet in diameter attached to the top end. Place the pole upright 10 yards in front of the trap. The trap should then be set to throw the target through the hoop centre.

A dumpy level, or similar, should be used to ensure that the correct measuring height is attained 10 yards from the trap, e.g., with rising ground from the trap it may be found that the ground has risen 2 feet at a point 10 yards from the trap. It will then be necessary to have this measuring pole 6 feet long and not 8 feet for that particular layout.

Target distance. With the trap set to throw a straight-away target when viewed from firing mark 3 a regular target shall travel a distance of 50 to 55 yards. A suitable post shall be set at this distance.

Angles. (a) The targets shall be thrown randomly within an area bounded by an angle of 22 degrees each side of an imaginary straight line drawn through the centre of firing mark No. 3 and projected past the centre of the pivot point of the trap when it is set to throw a straight-away target.

The trap shall be set at this angle to the left and to the right of this straight line for all registered events.

Note: These angles can be visibly checked by noting that with the trap set to throw an extreme left-hand target this would appear as a straight-away bird when viewed from firing mark No. 5 and for an extreme right-hand target as a straight-away bird when viewed from firing mark No. 1.

(b) To allow for unfavourable wind conditions, an additional tolerance of 10 degrees either side of the 22-degree angles left and right shall be considered as the boundary defining a widely different angle and two posts set at these further angles may be placed about 35 yards from the trap. Targets thrown within this area shall be considered to be within bounds.

The trap should be set so that the tip of the throwing arm, in the released position, is a minimum of 18 inches above ground level. Ideally the arm should be as near as possible to the trap-house roof.

30. Simultaneous discharge: when, for any cause, both barrels are discharged together or almost together. A simultaneous discharge shall be declared a malfunction and treated as such.

31. Stage: one part, division or section of a competition, usually twenty-five targets per competitor.

32. Squad: a number of competitors (usually five) whose names appear together on the same score-card to shoot the same stage on the same layout at the same time. Squads comprising more than five competitors are prohibited.

(a) They shall occupy the firing marks in the order in which their names are listed on the score-card.

(b) Competitors shall be arranged in squads of five except:

(i) when there are fewer than five competitors available;

(ii) when a competitor withdraws from a competition after it has begun;

(iii) when there is a shoot-off involving less than five competitors.

(c) The squad, when assembled and before any shooting commences at any stage, is permitted to view a regular target.

(d) The squad or a member of a squad may request to view a regular target after three consecutive broken targets have been thrown, or after a technical breakdown, or after a complaint regarding target flight, angle or distance has been upheld by the referee or jury after which shooting shall continue from the point at which the stage was interrupted.

(e) Members of the squad shall not move from their firing marks until the call of 'Change' or if so instructed by the referee.

(f) Members of the squad shall remain at the firing marks until the last shot of the stage is fired.

33. Targets. Targets used in all DTL registered events shall conform to the listed specification and colours.

Specifications: diameter: 109–111mm; height: 25–26mm; weight: 100–110 grams.

Colours permitted: all black, all white, all yellow, all orange; or the ring or dome of the target may be painted white, yellow or orange.

The colour of targets used should be that which is most visible against the shooting background.

34 Ties. All ties shall, whenever possible, be shot off in a manner the management deem best fitted to the equity of the competition. A competitor who is absent for a shoot-off shall lose by default.

Shoot-offs. (a) To decide ties, shoot-offs must take place to decide winners of championships, sections and classes, where there are titles, trophies or special prizes for such championship classes or sections.

(b) Shoot-offs shall normally take place over stages of twenty-five targets.

(c) Where there are less than five competitors involved in a shoot-off, No. 1 shall commence at No. 2 firing mark.

Add and Divide. Where cash prizes are awarded this system saves the necessity for shooting off. Method: The cash prizes to be awarded in the tie are added together and divided equally between the number of competitors in the tie e.g. assume a tie for second and third place. Add the prize money for second and third places together and divide this sum equally between the two competitors concerned.

35. Trap: a device constructed to throw properly

a clay target the prescribed height, angle and distance.

(a) Traps suitable for DTL:

(i) Any type of automatic angling trap that can properly throw targets to the specifications required for DTL may be used.

(ii) The trap must be capable of throwing targets at unknown angles, within the specifications for DTL and which cannot be predetermined.

(iii) Recommendation. Great care should be taken in selecting a suitable trap for DTL. Such machines have to cope with a great number of targets in a very short time. Choose a type that is capable of throwing a good target consistently and reliably.

(b) Types available:

(i) Manually operated. These machines are comparatively cheap to buy and, with good servicing, will give many years of service.

Installation: care must be taken to ensure a firm and level base for this trap and a strong base for the cocking lever. Follow the maker's instructions carefully.

Operation: these machines require two operators – one to load the machine and one to operate the cocking and release lever.

(ii) Electrically operated traps. These traps usually operate on a continuously angling basis. They are long lasting and trouble free.

Installation: this machine has only to be bolted down on to a suitable base, which should preferably be concrete, faced with wood.

Operation: these machines require two operators – one operator situated in the trap-house to load the target and one operator standing behind the shooter with the release button.

(iii) Electrically operated auto-loading traps. These machines are reliable, efficient and can give long and trouble-free service.

Installation: the machine need only be placed on a level surface and does not require more than nominal fixing, its weight being adequate to keep it in place.

Operation: these machines require only one operator if used with the push-button system. If used with acoustic release they may well operate perfectly without oper-

ators. Capacity is about 350 targets, adequate for two complete squads without refilling. Certain types of these machines can be used equally well for Automatic Ball Trap, the changeover taking perhaps five minutes.

Limitations: Traps with automatic loading, angling, cocking and firing devices are not suitable for Double Rise.

36. Unfinished competition.

(a) Should any competition fail to be completed due to extreme bad weather, darkness or major equipment failure, the competition may be curtailed or suspended.

(b) If curtailed, the award of prizes should be decided at some point in the competition equitable with fair play. It is recommended that a proportional refund should be made to each competitor.

(c) If suspended it shall be announced publicly at the suspended shoot a date at, and the terms under, which the competition shall continue. Such a date should be not more than four weeks from the date of the original competition.

(d) Any competitor who fails to attend on the new date set for the postponed competition shall forfeit all rights and standing in the competition. A refund of entry fee should be paid.

37. Widely different angle: a target that travels outside the prescribed extreme limits.

Double-Rise Shooting

38. Double Rise: in this type of shooting, two targets are released simultaneously and the shooter fires one shot at each target, scoring five points for killing both targets, two points for killing one target and zero for failing to kill either.

The trap angle does not alter as in Single-Rise shooting but is fixed near centrally to give the required flight and angles as required.

39. Regulations.

(a) General. Except where otherwise indicated, the general regulations given for Single-Rise events will normally apply. There are obvious differences in some instances and the following shall apply in respect of some particular regulations not quite so self-evident.

(b) Target angles. Set the trap to throw the

targets as near as possible equally angled one to the left and one to the right of the centre-line.

40. 'No Bird'.

(a)   The referee shall declare the pair 'No Bird' when:

(i) one target only is thrown;

(ii) two targets are killed with one shot;

(iii) either or both targets are thrown broken;

(iv) one target follows the other at an interval of time;

(v) an allowable misfire or malfunction occurs on either target;

(vi) the flight of either target appears irregular and the competitor has not fired a shot;

(vii) the shooter, having shot at and killed the first target, then refuses the second target which appears irregular.

In all such cases, a repeat pair will be thrown to determine the results of both shots.

(b)   (i) If the shooter, having shot at the first target and missed, refuses the second target, the pair shall be repeated to determine the result of the second shot only, the result of the first target being scored 'Lost'.

In such case, the shooter must be seen by the referee to shoot at or near the first target before shooting at the second target. If the shooter fails in this, the result shall be scored 'Lost and Lost'.

(ii) If a shooter shoots at both targets in flight, the result shall be scored.

(iv) One shot per target. A competitor shall shoot once only at each target. If a competitor misses the first target with the first shot and hits the same target with the second shot the referee shall declare both birds 'Lost'.

41. Ties: as for Single Rise, except that it is usual to shoot at the same number of targets per competitor as in a single stage of the competition.

Automatic Ball Trap

1. General

1.1   Application and scope of the technical regulations: At competitions where world records may be established and which are under the supervision of UIT, these regulations must be strictly adhered to.

1.2   The UIT recommends that in tournaments where world records cannot be established, such as regional or national competitions, the programmes prescribed by the UIT should be conducted in accordance with the rules of UIT.

1.3   It is the desire and attempt of the UIT to achieve uniformity in the conduct of shooting sports the world over. This is in the interest of the greater development of the sport and of the shooting fraternity.

1.4   These rules shall govern the conduct of all competitions under the supervision of the UIT. Any item which may not be specifically covered in these rules shall be decided by the competition jury in conjunction with the chief range officers.

1.5   Organization and execution of competitions: the host country or federation shall form an organizing committee for the general preparation and execution of the competitions. It shall consist of qualified individuals, representatives of the host country. One or more representatives of the UIT may be invited to serve as technical adviser(s) without voting rights.

1.6   The technical aspects of the individual events shall be the responsibility of the chief range officer. He shall have assistant range officers to aid him.

2. Public Affairs

2.1   Promotion and publicity shall be given all due consideration. Press, radio and television personnel shall be given every consideration and co-operation in keeping with the proper conduct of the competition.

They shall be given guidance and information in the placement of their equipment so that it will not interfere with the competitor or officials. Rooms with necessary office and communications equipment shall be made available for their use. Filming, recording and interviews should be done during the training periods or following competitions.

2.2   The classification and results control office shall prepare an accurate placing list

Waiting for a FITASC target with the gun in the compulsory down position.

immediately after a competition is completed and make copies available to the media.

2.3 In all competitions under the supervision of the UIT each competitor will bear a starting number on his back to aid in identifying. Starting numbers will not bear commercial advertising of any type.

2.4 Large score-boards should be conveniently placed where current results may be rapidly posted for the convenience of the public and press. The boards should be erected a sufficient distance away from the competition area so that loud discussions by spectators will not disturb competitors.

3. Equipment and Ammunition

3.1 General: all devices, ammunition or equipment which are not mentioned in these rules, or which are contrary to the spirit of these rules and regulations, are not allowed. The jury has the right to examine the shooter's equipment and apparel at any time there is reason to believe that these rules are being violated. It is the sole responsibility of the competitor to submit questionable equipment, ammunition or apparel for official inspection and approval in sufficient time prior to the beginning of a competition so that it will not inconvenience either the competitor or the officials. Team leaders are held equally responsible that their team members use equipment which is in accordance with these rules.

3.2 Guns: all types of shotguns, including automatics (self-loading), 12 gauge and smaller, may be used. No handicap will be allowed for use of guns of a smaller calibre than 12 gauge. Muzzle brakes, compensators, or other devices which serve like purposes are prohibited.

Ammunition: The length of the cartridge shall not exceed standard specifications of 70mm. Shot load shall not exceed 28 grams. Pellets shall be only spherical in shape, made of lead or alloy, and not larger than 2.5mm diameter. Black powder, tracer, incendiary or other forms of speciality-type cartridge are prohibited.

The referee or a jury member may remove an unfired cartridge from a shooter's gun for inspection.

4. Targets

4.1 Specifications: diameter: 110mm; height: 25–27mm; weight: 106 grams. Colours may be all black, all white or all yellow; or the full dome may be painted white or yellow; or a ring may be painted around the dome in white or yellow.

The colour of a target which is selected for a championship will be such that it is clearly visible against the background under all normal lighting conditions.

The colour and country of manufacture of the targets will be included in all programmes for competitions which are under the supervision of the UIT.

4.2 Random sample of the targets, twenty targets taken from different cartons, will be examined by the technical committee prior to any competition to ascertain that they meet the specifications. Organizers who are in doubt about their targets should submit samples to the UIT sufficiently in advance of a championship to allow corrections to be made if the targets do not meet the requirements.

5. Positions

5.1 The shooter shall stand with both feet entirely within the boundaries of his station. He may not move from his position until the shooter to the right has shot at a regular target, except when the shooter has fired at his own regular target on Station 5. When a shooter has completed his shots on Station 5 he must immediately proceed to Station 1, being careful he does not disturb the shooters who are on the line as he walks past.

6. Range Standards

6.1 General: ranges which are constructed in the northern hemisphere should be laid out so that the direction of shooting is toward a north to north-easterly area. This places the sun to the back of the shooter as much as possible during the shooting day.

6.2 The trap pit: a trap-house will be constructed, the top of the roof of which will be on the same elevation as the surface of the shooting stations. Interior measurements of the trap-house should be approximately 4 metres from side to side × 2 metres from front to rear × 2 metres from floor to the inside of the roof. These dimensions will allow freedom of movement of working personnel and sufficient storage space for competition targets.

6.3   The shooting stations: the shooting stations will be arranged on an arc measured and drawn at 15 metres to the behind of the trap-house, measured from the front edge and centre of the roof.

Station 3 will be centred on an imaginary line drawn through the centre of the trap-house to the rear and perpendicular to the front of the house. Stations 1, 2, 4 and 5 will be located on the arc on points measured 3 metres and 6 metres to the left and right of the centre-line respectively.

6.4   The trap (throwing device): the pit shall be equipped with a single, multi-oscillating (in vertical and horizontal directions) mechanical or electrically operated trap. It may be either manually or automatically loaded. Targets may be released manually, electrically or microphone-electrically. The trap will be so constructed and mounted that it will throw at random and at continuously changing angles and elevations, an unbroken target within the vertical and horizontal limits stated within these rules.

6.5   Target distances, angles and elevations. The trap shall be so adjusted that in calm weather:

(a)   with a throwing elevation of 2 metres, at 10 metres forward of the pit, a properly released target will carry 75 metres (+ or − 5 metres) if measured over level ground;

(b)   the height of the target's path above the level of the trap-house roof and 10 metres forward of the trap shall be at least 1 metre and not exceed 4 metres;

(c)   the targets shall be thrown within an area bounded by angles of not less than 30 degrees nor more than 45 degrees right and left of the imaginary centre-line drawn through the centre of the trap-house and Station 3. The horizontal angles will be measured from the front edge of the trap-house;

(d)   the traps must be adjusted and examined by the jury each day before the shooting begins.

One trial target shall be thrown for each squad before the first shooter begins his series.

7.   Courses of Fire

7.1   Individual: a competition consists of 200 targets shot in eight series of twenty-five targets each. These may be shot in two days at 100 targets each day or in three days at seventy-five + seventy-five + fifty targets. Under extremely crowded conditions a competition may be scheduled for four days at fifty targets per day.

7.2   Teams: the number of shooters per team is regulated by the UIT General Regulations. The team score shall be determined by the totals from the results of the individual scores over the first 150 targets (first six series) fired.

7.3   Women and juniors: individual competitions only consisting of 150 targets fired according to 7.1 above.

8.   Time Limits

8.1   It is the shooter's responsibility to be on the proper layout at the proper time with sufficient ammunition and necessary equipment.

8.2   A shooter must position himself, load his gun and call for his target within fifteen seconds after the shooter to his left has fired at a regular target or after the field referee has given the signal to start firing in the event of delay.

8.3   After the shooter has called for his target, it shall be released immediately, allowing for human reaction time to press a button if the release is manual-electrical or mechanical. When targets are released by microphone-electrical means, a delay factor of 0.2 seconds shall be built into the system to more nearly simulate the human reaction time when targets are released by hand.

8.4   If shooting is interrupted within a series for more than five minutes, the squad is allowed to view one unbroken, regular target before commencing the competition again.

9.   Competition Regulations and Range Procedures

9.1   Squadding: a squad normally consists of six competitors drawn at random from the entry list. In international competitions the shooters of each country are distributed over the various squads. Drawings are made separately for each day at a time announced in advance, thereby permitting the delegates of the participating nations to be present. In the interest of expediency the jury may complete the drawing without reference to the delegates. Attendance at the drawing by the delegates is optional. The squadding list shall be posted at noon each day prior to the day of the specified match.

9.2 At the beginning of each series the first five shooters in each squad will take positions on Stations 1 to 5, the Shooter No. 6 will remain ready behind the number 1 position to move in as soon as Shooter No. 1 has shot. After Shooter No. 1 has fired at a regular target, he is to prepare to move to Station 2 as soon as the shooter on the post has fired, and so on.

When the shooter on post 5 has fired he must immediately move around the rear of the firing line and return to post 1, continuing the rotation until each shooter has fired at twenty-five targets. No member of a squad, having shot on one station, shall proceed towards the next station in such a way as to interfere with another shooter or the match personnel.

Targets will be thrown on a completely random basis with each shooter required to fire at every regular target which is released on his call.

9.3 Once shooting has been started it shall continue without interruption according to the programme except for mechanical breakdown or other emergencies determined by the chief range officer and the jury. In the event of bad weather of obviously short duration the chief range officer with the jury's agreement may halt the shooting temporarily.

9.4 Regular target: any target which is thrown on the shooter's call according to Rule 6.5 is deemed a regular target.

Irregular target: any target which deviates from the specifications of Rule 6.5 as to angle and elevation and distance shall be deemed to be irregular. A broken target is not considered an irregular target.

Broken target: any target which is not whole, according to Rule 4.1. A shooter who receives a broken target must repeat his shot on a regular target regardless of whether he hit or missed the broken target if he shot.

9.5 Malfunctions.

(a) Any shotgun which cannot be safely fired, which 'doubles' automatically (double-barrelled, pump or semi-automatic) or which fails to eject due to a mechanical defect is considered to be disabled under this rule. A shotgun which fires automatically, owing to a faulty manipulation by the shooter, is not considered disabled.

A shotgun once declared disabled is not to be used again in the same tournament until the problem has been corrected and ruled safe by a competent armourer and accepted by the jury.

(b) Malfunction of firearm: failure of a gun to function properly due to a mechanical defect or defective ammunition will be declared a malfunction. Functional failures caused by improper manual manipulation by the user will not be considered as a malfunction. Failure to place the cartridge in the proper chamber of the gun is considered the fault of the shooter and is not allowable as a malfunction.

(c) Malfunction of ammunition: failure of ammunition to fire or function properly, i.e. failure to fire providing firing pin indentation is clearly noticeable; or firing of primer only, where powder charge has been omitted or not ignited, which is characterized by a very weak report and absence of noticeable recoil, are characteristics of defective ammunition.

Components of the load remaining in the barrel shall be considered as evidence of defective ammunition but not a requirement. Wrong-size cartridges and empty shells in the chamber shall not be considered as defective ammunition.

(d) In all cases of disablement or malfunction of gun or ammunition, and upon the decision of the referee that this has not been caused by the shooter himself and that the gun is not repairable quickly enough, the shooter has the option of using another gun if one can be obtained without delay (within three minutes after the referee has declared the gun disabled). If not, the shooter may leave the squad and finish the remaining shots of the round at a time decided by the referee or when a vacancy occurs and the shooter obtains the permission of the referee. If the gun is repaired before the end of the round the shooter may be allowed to rejoin his squad with the permission of the referee.

The shooter is allowed a total of two malfunctions per round of twenty-five targets regardless of whether he has changed his gun or ammunition.

The third and subsequent malfunctions of either gun or ammunition are considered excessive. Each regular target attempted thereafter on which an excessive malfunction occurs shall be declared 'Lost'.

9.6   Penalties.

(a)   It is the responsibility of the shooter to be present on the proper field at the proper time with all his equipment and ready to shoot. If a shooter is not present on the line when his name is called, the referee will announce the shooter's name loudly three times within one minute. If the shooter does not appear within this time the shooting will commence without him. The shooter will be marked absent on the official score-sheet. He may be permitted to shoot the missed round at a time and on the field decided by the chief range officer with the agreement of the jury. The shooter will be penalized with a deduction of three targets from the result of a late-fired round.

(b)   All other violations of these rules shall incur a warning on the first offence in a round of twenty-five targets. The second and subsequent violations in the same round shall incur a deduction of one hit from the result of that round for each violation.

(c)   Other penalties according to specific rules.

9.7   Unsportsmanlike conduct, or deliberate attempts to evade the spirit of these rules, may incur a warning, a penalty of elimination from the competition based upon the decision of the jury or the jury of appeal if one has been appointed for the competition.

9.8   A target is declared 'Dead' when it is thrown and shot at according to the rules, breaking a visible piece from it by the shot.

9.9   A target is declared 'Lost' when:

(a)   it is not hit during its flight;

(b)   it is only dusted (no visible piece falls);

(c)   the shooter does not fire at a regular target for which he has called;

(d)   the shooter is not able to fire his gun because he has not released the safety, forgotten to load or failed to cock his gun;

(e)   the first shot is a miss and the shooter fails to fire his second shot because he forgot to place a second cartridge in the gun or to release the stop on the magazine on an automatic shotgun, or because the safety has slipped back to the 'safe' position by the recoil of the first shot;

(f)   a malfunction of the gun or the ammunition occurs and the shooter opens the gun or touches the safety before the referee has examined the gun;

(g)   it is the third or subsequent malfunction of the gun or the ammunition by the same shooter in a 25-target round.

9.10   A 'No Bird' is to be declared and another target allowed whether or not the competitor has fired:

(a)   if the target is thrown before the shooter has called;

(b)   if the target is not thrown immediately after his call and the shooter lowers his gun. (*See* Rule 8.)

9.11   In case of malfunction or misfire not caused by the shooter himself, another target shall be allowed (*See* Rule 9.5) if:

(a)   the competitor's first shot misfires and he does not fire the second shot. If the second shot is fired, the result is scored;

(b)   the first shot is a miss and the competitor's second shot misfires. In this case, the first shot on the new target must miss the target and the shooter must attempt to hit the target with his second shot. If the target is hit with the first shot it is scored 'Lost'.

Note: a competitor using a double-barrelled gun with a selective single trigger may be requested, before the beginning of a competition, to make a declaration as to which barrel he is going to fire first. If he fails to make this declaration, he forfeits the advantage of a new target according to this rule.

9.12   The referee may declare a 'No Bird' and allow another target if:

(a)   the shooter has been materially disturbed, such as being struck by a piece of target from a neighbouring range, sudden appearance of trap boys, or sudden and unnatural loud noises at the moment that he has called for his target.

If the shooter fires both shots at a regular target he may not claim interference or disturbance. (*See* note below);

(b) another competitor has fired at his target.

Note: The referee shall consult with the assistant referees if a repeat target is to be thrown under this rule and he shall make the final decision.

9.13 If both shots are discharged simultaneously the result shall be scored regardless of whether the target was hit or missed.

9.14 A shot is counted as not fired if:

(a) a competitor shoots out of turn;

(b) a shot is discharged before the competitor has called for his target. However, if the target is thrown and the competitor fires his second shot, the result must be scored.

Note: If the shooter has a malfunction on the first shot and fires his second shot, the result shall be scored.

10. Range Controls

10.1 All guns shall be handled with the greatest care. Conventional double-barrel guns are to be carried with the breech open. Magazine guns are to be carried with the breech open and muzzle pointing straight upward or down at the ground. Straps and slings are not allowed on guns in this competition.

When a shooter is not carrying his gun, it must be placed in a gun rack with the muzzle up, after having ascertained that the gun is clear. No individual is allowed to touch another's gun without the owner's permission.

10.2 All guns must be carried open when moving between Stations 1, 2, 3, 4 and 5 on the firing line. When moving from Station 5 to Station 1, the gun must be open and completely unloaded.

10.3 Shooting and sighting practice may be done only on the shooting stations. It is expressly prohibited to place a gun to the shoulder and practise swinging behind the firing lines. Shots may be fired only when it is the shooter's turn and after his target has been thrown. It is forbidden to sight at another competitor's targets.

10.4 It is forbidden to sight or shoot at live birds or animals.

10.5 Cartridges may not be placed into any part of the gun until the shooter is standing on his station facing the traps with the gun pointed to the flight area and the referee has given permission to load. Magazine guns must be blocked so that it is not possible to place more than one cartridge into the magazine at one time. A shooter is not allowed to close his gun before it is the turn of the competitor to his left to shoot.

10.6 If the target is not thrown immediately after the shooter has called, the shooter is to signify that he refuses the target by quickly lowering the gun from his shoulder.

10.7 The shooter is not allowed to turn from the shooting station before his gun is opened. When an irregular target is thrown or the shooting is interrrupted, the guns shall be opened. No gun shall be closed until the order to continue has been given.

10.8 In the event of a misfire or other malfunction, the shooter shall remain standing, with the gun pointed to the target flight area, without opening the gun or touching the safety until the referee has inspected the gun.

10.9 The shooting shall be carried out without interruption according to the programme. The shooter shall restrict his conversation to calling for his targets, reporting 'Ready' when asked, signifying a protest if necessary and answering questions of the referee.

10.10 The referee or his assistants, under the supervision of the jury, are responsible to see that the safety precautions are adhered to, that unauthorized persons are expelled from the range and that the puller and the assistant referees have an unobstructed view of all the shooting stations and the area in front of the trap pit.

11. Referee

11.1 (a) The shooting on each layout shall be conducted by a referee with wide experience in clay-pigeon shooting and a sound knowledge of shotguns. His main function is to make immediate decisions regarding hit or missed targets, and he must give a distinct signal for each missed target.

(b) The referee shall be aided by two assistant

(side) referees. Assistant referees are normally appointed in rotation from among the competitors, preferably from those who have shot in the preceding squad. All competitors are obligated, upon request, to function as assistant referees. The referee may accept substitutes at his own discretion. The primary function of the assistant referee is to give, immediately after a shot, a signal by raising his hand or a small flag if he considers a target 'Lost'. The assistant referee closest to the large field score-board is responsible for checking the entry of results during the shooting.

(c) The referee is responsible for making immediate and accurate decisions regarding 'No Bird', repeat targets, 'Dead' or 'Lost' targets, irregular targets or other conditions. Whenever possible the referee shall call or signal a 'No Bird' before the shooter has fired his first shot.

(d) The referee shall make all decisions himself. If any of the assistant referees is in disagreement, it is his duty to signal and advise the referee of this. The referee may then make his final decision.

(e) Decisions of the referee may be appealed against in so far as the interpretation and application of the rules is concerned. The decision of the referee is final in so far as hit or missed targets or irregular targets are concerned. These latter decisions may not be appealed against.

11.2 Jury. At all competitions under the supervision of the UIT and where world records may be established, a jury shall be appointed. The jury shall consist of not less than three nor more than five members.

The list of jury members shall be submitted to the Secretariat, UIT, for review by the technical committee and approval by the executive committee. The chairman of the jury will normally be a qualified representative of the host country. The jury makes decisions by majority vote. In urgent cases, two unanimous members of the jury may make decisions in consultation with the referee. The jury is responsible for supervising and ensuring that the operating personnel and referees are adhering to the rules and applying them impartially. The jury is responsible for deciding conflicts which cannot be resolved by the referee.

11.3 It is the duty of the jury to:

(a) verify that the shooting ranges and organization plans are according to the regulations of the UIT and the approved programme;

(b) ensure that the competition rules and the programme are followed by the operating personnel and participants;

(c) make decisions in cases when situations cannot be resolved by the referee or organizers;

(d) make decisions regarding penalties and sanctions against competitors who do not adhere to the rules and conduct themselves in an unsportsmanlike manner;

(e) arrange a working agreement with the other jury members whereby at least two members of the jury will be present on the ranges at all times, one of whom should be within immediate calling distance of any referee.

11.4 The jury's decisions cannot be appealed against unless a jury of appeal has been appointed for the competitors by the UIT.

12. Team Officials

12.1 It is the responsibility of the team leader to be thoroughly familiar with the competition regulations and the programmes in which he is entering competitors.

The team leader is further responsible for ensuring that his competitors present themselves at their shooting stations at the proper time with proper equipment. If there is any doubt about the eligibility of any item it should be presented to the proper officials prior to the competition for examination. If a team is small and does not have a non-competing leader, one of the shooters must be designated as the team leader before the competitions begin.

12.2 Although coaching is not allowed in UIT competitions many teams have such a member in their teams. This individual is not permitted inside the shooting areas unless he has been appointed to some other competition function, in which case he is prohibited from serving his team members while in the competition official capacity.

12.3 Team composition is determined by the UIT according to its constitution and general regulations, in conjunction with the host coun-

Ian Coley explains the rudiments of gun handling to a lady pupil.

try. In the case of the Olympic games, team composition is determined by the IOC, UIT and the host country.

13.   *Results Office Operations*

13.1   It is the duty of the results office to:
(a)   prepare a list of competitors and assign numbers to each;
(b)   assist in the drawing of lots to squad the competitors;
(c)   prepare score-sheets for each squad;
(d)   ensure that the proper score-sheet is with the correct squad on the correct layout;
(e)   receive and verify addition of scores on official sheets from each squad as they complete the series;
(f)   tabulate scores in order of merit and post preliminary results on the public bulletin board immediately, and finalize official results as early as possible daily;
(g)   prepare a preliminary results bulletin for distribution each day;
(h)   prepare and publish a final results bulletin immediately after the completion of the competition and the close of any allowable protest period;
(i)   send ten copies of the official results bulletin and any reports to the Secretariat of the UIT within thirty days of the completion of the competition.

14.   *Scoring*

14.1   Scoring is done officially on each layout for each round of twenty-five targets based on the decision of the referee. In UIT supervised events, where world records may be established, scores will be kept on each field by three separate persons, two of whom will post on permanent cards and be positioned on each side of the field to the rear of the firing line while the third will maintain a larger board for the benefit of the shooters and spectators. Each scorer will mark his card or board independently. At the conclusion of each round, the results should be identical.

If there is any discrepancy in one score-keeper's posting, the two which are alike shall be the official score. If none of the posted results compare, the large public board will be the deciding one. It is the duty of the assistant referee nearest the large board to ensure that the scorer is posting the referee's decisions correctly.

14.2   After a squad completes a stage and the scores have been verified the referee and each shooter must sign or initial the sheet so that it may be quickly returned to the results office. Failure to sign the sheet before it leaves the layout eliminates all right to protest of scores which are posted as a final results from the sheets.

14.3   The decision of the referee is final as to whether a target is 'Dead' or 'Lost'. The referee, when in doubt, should consult the assistant referees, then make his final decision.

Universal Trench

Shooting Range

Art. 1.   An international shooting range for Universal Trench comprises five traps which are placed in a trench, fitted with a fixed or hinged roof.

The five traps shall be arranged in a straight line on supports firmly sealed, aligned and perfectly in position on the throwing line platform of each of them. There is:
(a)   A horizontal distance of 1 metre minimum and 1.25 metres maximum between the centres of the two clay targets arranged on two adjacent traps ready to be thrown.
(b)   A vertical distance of 0.5 metres between the centre of each clay target measured from the upper tip of the upper surface of the trench roof, it being understood that this surface of the trench roof corresponds exactly to the level of the shooting station and that each trap is set for the highest trajectory permitted (4 metres).

Shooting Station

At the same level as the roof of the trench, and 15 metres behind the traps, are the shooting stations equipped with a bench or stand on which the shooters may replace their cartridges.

The shooting stations are five squares 1.0×1.0m and shall be arranged in a straight line parallel to the five trench traps. There must be 15 metres measured horizontally between the front line of the shooting station and that passing through the centres of the targets in position for throwing on the trench traps.

The axis of the central Station 3 must pass through the exact centre of the clay target of trap 3 and be directly perpendicular to the alignment of the five traps.

The shooting stations being set out so that there are two on the left of Station 3 and two on the right, shall be spaced out at 2.5 metres from axis to axis, in order to leave intervals of 1.5 metres width between each of the shooting stations.

Art. 2. As is mentioned in Art. 3, the trajectories of the targets thrown by the five trench traps can be modified in order to vary the shooting conditions. However, the regular trajectories must meet the scheme conditions when there is no wind:

(a) The trench traps must be fitted with devices permitting independent modifications: the power of projection (length of throw), the orientations and the height of the trajectory of the clay targets. They shall be fitted with graduated marking devices enabling by simple wording to proceed to the various settings provided for in accordance with the published schemes.

(b) Each trap, having been set thus, shall be solidly fixed so that the trajectory obtained cannot be altered whilst the event is in progress. For the same reason, the position of the clay target in position on the trap and ready to be thrown must always be exactly the same. If required, each trap shall be fitted with a device permitting only one precise position where the clay target shall be placed to be thrown. If it is adjustable, this device must be firmly locked.

(c) The various setting devices on each trap (projection, power, orientation, height of trajectory and, should the situation arise, initial position of the clay target) must be fitted with holes enabling control seals to be fitted.

Art. 3. During the course of a competition, the trajectories of each trench trap will be modified each day. The new settings shall be decided by the jury and effected before the shooting commences. The modification made to the trajectory of each trap shall be according to another of the set schemes.

When the new settings have been carried out, a trial target shall be thrown from each trap and all the setting devices shall be sealed.

Art. 4. The traps must be released by an electrical or mechanical device placed in position where the operator can see and hear the shooters. In all international competitions, an electrical selector will be used so that all the shooters receive identical targets. The selector must be changed by one notch after each round of five birds and before the shooter from Station 1 requests his target.

Art. 5. The clay targets shall have a diameter of 11cm, a height of 25–28.5mm and a weight of 100–110 grams. In international competitions, the targets must be of an approved make.

Art. 6. The shooting range shall be laid out in such a way and the targets shall be of such a colour that the targets are clearly visible against the background under all normal light conditions.

Organizing of Competitions

Art. 7. As a rule, shooting should be carried out in squads consisting of six shooters. The management should, if possible, fill vacancies with proficient shooters not taking part in the competition.

Art. 8. In international competitions, the shooters of each country shall be spread over the various squads. The management shall draw up a plan for the distribution, whereafter lots are drawn separately for each day at a time announced in advance, thereby permitting the delegates of the participating nations to be present. Firing order within each shooting squad is decided by new ballot each day and the order of the shooting shall be posted.

Art. 9. At the beginning of the competition, five shooters shall be ready to shoot, one at each shooting station. The sixth shooter must be ready to take the place of competitor No. 1. When the competitor at Station 1 has fired at the first target, he is to prepare himself for taking up position at Station 2 as soon as the shooter at Station 2 has fired and so on.

Art. 10. Each stage consists of twenty-five targets. In smaller events it may be decided that the stages shall comprise fewer targets.

Art. 11. It shall be so arranged that the shooters are unable to pre-determine from which of the five traps in the group the targets will be thrown. Releasing, however, to be performed according to a system whereby each shooter receives an even distribution of targets thrown.

Art. 12. The shooting shall be carried out with no other intervals than those decided in the programme or caused by technical difficulties. In exceptional cases, however, the referee may – with the jury's agreement – interrupt the shooting if sudden bad weather of obviously short duration arises.

Art. 13. If a shooter is not present when his name is called, the referee must call the number and name of the shooter three times loudly within a period of one minute. If he does not appear then, the shooting shall start without him.

Art. 14. Any malfunction of a trap during the shooting must be indicated to the referee who decides whether the competition must be interrupted or continued with the remaining traps. At the end of the series, the case is brought before the jury. When a trap has been repaired or adjusted, a new trial target shall be thrown from all of the traps.

Art. 15. During international competitions, the scores shall be recorded by three people. One of these shall have the added function of recording each malfunction of gun or ammunition. another must record the scores upon a large board visible to the shooters and spectators. Immediately after each round, the scores shall be compared and any disputes shall be decided for each target before the shooters leave the shooting range. If one of the scores does not correspond to the other, only that corresponding to the board will be valid.

The scores of the rounds shall be read aloud, so that they may be heard by the shooters. Each shooter must check his final score himself, before leaving the shooting range.

Referees and Jury

Art. 16. The shooting shall be conducted by a referee with wide experience in clay-target shooting and who should normally have a referee's licence. His main function is to make immediate decisions regarding hit or missed targets and he is to give a distinct signal for each missed target.

Art. 17. The referee shall be aided by two assistant judges. Usually these are to be appointed in rotation by the referee from among the competitors, and preferably amongst those who have fired in the previous squad. All competitors are obliged upon request to function as assistant judges, but the referee has the right to accept substitutes if he thinks fit (*see also* Art. 68).

The main function of an assistant judge is to give, immediately after a shot, a signal by raising his hand if he considers a target 'Lost'. The assistant judge closest to the scoring-board can check the entry of the results during the shooting.

Art. 18. The referee is to make an immediate decision as to whether a repeat target is to be thrown as a result of an irregular target or some other condition (*see* Art. 31, 32 and 34). He must, if possible, call 'No Bird' before the shooter has fired his first shot.

Art. 19. The referee shall always make decisions himself. If any of the assistant judges is in disagreement, it is his duty to raise his hand and advise the referee of this. The referee is then to make his final decision.

The Jury

Art. 20. Providing no other decision has been made, there shall be a jury for international competitions, consisting of a representative from each country, with the organizing country's representative as chairman.

If more than five countries participate, the representatives shall appoint a jury consisting of five members. The jury makes decisions by majority. The chairman's vote decides equal votes. The jury can make valid decisions when the chairman and two members are present. In urgent cases two members of the jury may make decisions, after consultation with the referee if their decision is unanimous.

Art. 21. It is the duty of the jury:
(a) to see before shooting begins that the ranges conform with regulations (*see* Art. 1 and

6) and that arrangements in general are suitable and correct;

(b) to see during the shooting that the rules are adhered to and check guns, ammunition and target by random test or other suitable procedure;

(c) to make the necessary decisions in connection with technical defects or other disturbances in the shooting if these are not taken care of by the referee;

(d) to deal with protests (*see* the last paragraph of Art. 49);

(e) to make decisions regarding penalties if a shooter does not adhere to the rules or deports himself in an unsportsmanlike manner;

(f) to agree upon a working arrangement whereby at least two members of the jury are always present on the range, one of them to be in the immediate vicinity of the referee.

Art. 22. The jury's decision cannot be appealed against, unless a special jury of appeal has been appointed for the competition.

Guns and Ammunition

Art. 23. All guns, including automatic models, 12 gauge and smaller, may be used for shooting. Compensators or similar devices which may disturb the competitors are not allowed. No handicap will be given to competitors using guns with a calibre smaller than 12.

Art. 24. The length of the shell is not to exceed 70mm. The shot is not to be larger than 2.5mm (No. 6) in diameter and the load of shot is not to exceed 28 grams. It is not allowed to use black powder or tracer cartridges.

Art. 25. In case of malfunction of the gun and upon decision of the referee that this has not been caused by the shooter himself and that the gun is not repairable quickly enough, the shooter has the option of using another gun if such one can be secured without delay. If not, he will leave his squad and finish the remaining shots of the series at a later time decided by the referee or when a vacancy occurs and the shooter has the permission of the referee. If his gun is repaired before the end of the stage, the shooter is allowed to join the squad with the permission of the referee.

In the event of another malfunction of the gun or ammunition which results in the shot not being fired, and it is not the fault of the shooter, he has the possibility of continuing with the same gun or changing it.

He will have the right to a new target three times during each series of twenty-five in all cases of malfunctioning provided for in this regulation, regardless of whether he has changed his gun or not. The fourth and subsequent malfunctions will be considered 'Lost' (*see* Art. 30).

A shot will be considered as 'No Bird' (allowable malfunction) if the primer does not ignite after having been struck and shows signs of percussion.

Shooting Rules

Art. 26. Two shots may be fired at each target.

Art. 27. Shooting Position: standing in any position. The shooter must stand on the shooting station, with his feet behind the front line.

Art. 28. When the competitor is ready to shoot, he orders the target to be thrown by shouting 'Pull' or some other word of command, after which the target shall be thrown immediately.

Art. 29. The target is declared 'Killed' when it is thrown and shot at according to the rules and if at least one visible piece of it is broken or the target is shot partly or entirely to pieces.

Art. 30. The target is declared 'Lost' when:

(a) it is not hit during its flight;

(b) it is only dusted;

(c) the shooter does not fire at a target which he has called;

(d) the shooter is unable to fire because he has not released the safety catch, forgotten to load or cock his gun or if it has been insufficiently closed;

(e) the first shot is a miss and the shooter fails to fire his second shot because he forgot to place a second cartridge or to release the stop on the magazine of an automatic shotgun, or because the safety catch has slipped back to 'safe' by the concussion of the first shot or again if the second cartridge comes unsealed and empties from the effect of the recoil;

(f) there is a case of misfire or malfunction of the gun and the shooter opens the gun or

Former World FITASC Sporting Champion, John Bidwell, waits for a target with the gun out of his shoulder, as the FITASC rules stipulate.

touches the safety catch before the referee has examined the gun;

(g)   it is the fourth or subsequent malfunction of the gun or the ammunition by the same shooter in a stage;

(h)   the shot is not fired due to some reason which does not entitle the shooter to a repeat target.

Art. 31.   The target is considered a 'No Bird' and a new target shall be thrown whether or not the competitor has fired if:

(a)   the target breaks when released;

(b)   the trajectory is irregular (the target flutters, has insufficient velocity, etc.);

(c)   two or more targets are thrown simultaneously;

(d)   the target is of a colour manifestly different from that of the other targets used in the competition.

Art. 32.   'No Bird' is to be declared and another target allowed if the shooter has not fired if:

(a)   the target is thrown before the shooter has given the command;

(b)   the target is not thrown immediately after the command, and the shooter clearly raised his gun.

Art. 33.   In case of misfire or malfunction not caused by the shooter himself, another target shall be allowed if:

(a)   the competitor's first shot misfires and he does not fire the second shot. (If the second shot is fired, the result of this is to count.);

(b)   the first shot is a miss and the competitor's second shot misfires. In this case the first shot on the new target must be fired in the air and outside the line of flight. If hit with the first shot the target is lost. Shooters using a double-barrel gun with a selective single trigger are invited to make a declaration before the beginning of the competition as to what barrel they are going to fire first.

Failing this official declaration they may not have the advantage of a new target (*see* Art. 30 (f) and 45).

Art. 34.   The referee may also order a new target to be thrown if:

(a)   the shooter has been materially disturbed;

(b)   another competitor shoots at the same target;

(c)   the referee due to some special reason

cannot decide whether the target was killed or lost. (*see* Art. 19, 48 and 49). The referee must always consult his assistants before allowing a new target in these circumstances.

Art. 35.   The repeat target must be thrown along the same trajectory as the 'No Bird' but the shooter cannot in any event refuse it, even if he has the impression that the target was thrown from another trap.

Art. 36.   If both shots are fired simultaneously, the result is to count.

Art. 37.   A shot is counted as not fired if:

(a)   the shooter shoots out of turn (*see* Art. 39, 54);

(b)   the shooter fires when it is his turn but before having given the command. If, however, the target is thrown and the competitor fires his second shot, the result of this to count. If the shooter has a malfunction during his first shot and fires the second shot, the result will count.

Rules of Conduct

Art. 38.   All guns, even when empty, must be handled with the greatest care. The guns must be carried open; as for magazine guns, the breech must be open and the gun carried with the muzzle pointed upwards or downwards. Straps on guns are not allowed. When a shooter puts his gun aside it must be placed vertically in a gun-stand or another place intended for this purpose. It is forbidden to touch another competitor's gun without the owner's consent. All guns must be carried open between Station 1 and 5 and must be carried open and unloaded when moving from Station 5 to Station 1.

Art. 39.   Shooting and sighting may only be practised at shooting stations. Shots may only be fired when it is the shooter's turn and the target has been thrown. It is forbidden to sight or shoot at another competitor's targets. It is also forbidden to sight or shoot at live animals or birds.

Art. 40.   At roll-call the shooter must be ready to shoot immediately and take with him the ammunition and equipment which he needs for the round.

Art. 41.   The shooter shall remain at the shooting station until the competitor on his right-hand side has fired. The shooter at Station 5 must go immediately to Station 1. After the shooters have fired their last shot in the stage, they are to remain standing at their stations until the last man in the squad has fired and the referee has announced 'Finished'.

Art. 42.   It is not allowed to put cartridges in the gun before the shooter is standing at the shooting station, his gun pointed at the flight area and before the referee has given the signal to begin the shooting.

Magazine guns must be constructed in such a way that it is not possible to load with more than two cartridges. The shooter must not close his gun before the competitor on his left is ready to shoot.

Art. 43.   If the target is not thrown immediately after the command has been given, the shooter is to denote that he refrains from shooting by clearly raising his gun (*see* Art. 32 (b)).

Art. 44.   The shooter must not turn from the shooting station before the gun is opened. When a 'No Bird' is thrown or the shooting is interrupted, the gun shall be opened. It is not to be closed again until shooting can continue.

Art. 45.   In case of misfire or malfunction of gun or ammunition, the shooter shall remain standing with the gun pointed to the flight area without opening the gun or touching the safety catch until the referee has inspected the gun (*see* Art. 30 and 33).

Art. 46.   The shooting shall be carried out without interruptions, and the shooters are only to give the necessary words of command, report 'Ready' or possibly 'Protest' and answer the referee's questions.

Art. 47.   The referee or his assistants, under the supervision of the jury, are to see that the regulations are adhered to, that unauthorized persons are expelled from the range and that the shooters have an unobstructed view of all the shooting stations.

Protests

Art. 48.   If the shooter or team captain disagrees with the referee's decision regarding a shot, protest must be made immediately upon the occurrence of the incident, by raising the arm and saying 'Protest' or 'Appeal.' The referee shall then interrupt the shooting and, after having heard the opinion of the assistant judges, make known his decision. It is forbidden to pick up a clay pigeon in order to find out if it has been hit or not.

Art. 49.   The referee's decision can be appealed against verbally or in writing to the jury. At least one jury member must always stay near the referee to be able to receive such protests. If the jury finds the protest justified, it can give the referee directions for future decisions, or appoint a new referee, or change his decision inasmuch as this does not concern hits, misses or irregular targets, when the referee's decision is final.

Art. 50.   If a shooter or team captain is of the opinion that the score which is read aloud when the stage is finished is incorrect, he should make his protest verbally to the referee immediately. The referee shall then as soon as possible – in the presence of the scorers – examine the scoresheets, after which he is to make his decision. If the person protesting is not satisfied with the decision, a short, written protest shall be handed to the jury.

Art. 51.   If a competitor, team captain or official observes anything which does not conform with these rules, he must report this to the referee or a member of the jury. The referee must, if he cannot take immediate necessary measures, refer the reporter to a member of the jury. The referee's decision can be appealed against to the jury in the form of a short written protest.

Penalties and Other Consequences

Art. 52.   All shooters are obliged to acquaint themselves with these rules in so far as they apply to the shooters and the shooting. By taking part in the competitions, they bind themselves to penalties and other consequences which may arise and result from the violation of any the rules or of the orders of the referees.

Art. 53.   If the shooter uses guns or ammunition which are not in accordance with Art. 23 and 24, all shots fired with such guns or such ammunition are to be counted as lost. If the jury finds that the fault has been committed with intent, it can in consequence hereof exclude the shooter from the competition.

If the jury finds that the shooter could not reasonably be aware of the fault and that he, through the fault, has attained no essential advantage, it can decide to approve of the shooting results, providing the fault is corrected as soon as the shooter has become aware of it.

Art. 54. The violation of Art. 27, 38, 39, 41, 42, 44 and 46 normally incur a warning in the first instance by the referee or a member of the jury. The jury may fine the shooter one bird on repeated violations or major transgressions, and in aggravated circumstances may exclude the shooter from the stage concerned or from the whole match.

Art. 55. If the shooter is not present at roll-call after three calls, he will be fined three targets deducted on the first three kills at his next stage. The jury may give him the opportunity to shoot the remaining targets later on, at a time to be fixed by the referee.

If a shooter leaves his group for one of the reasons provided for in Art. 13 and 25, one kill will be deducted from his score for each interruption and he will be allowed to shoot the remaining targets later.

The shooter who refuses to take his turn as assistant referee when designated will lose one kill.

Art. 56. Should the jury find that a shooter intentionally delays the shooting or deports himself in an unsportsmanlike manner, it may give him a warning or fine him one target or exclude him from the match.

Art. 57. When the jury fines a shooter one target and this decision does not refer to a special target, the first kill after the decision has been made known is to be counted as lost. If the shooter has completed the day's shooting, the target shall be deducted from the score of the last stage.

Tie-Shooting

Art. 58. If two or more shooters obtain the same score in a championship competition, precedence for the first three places shall be decided by tie-shooting in 25-target stages until a difference in the scores occurs. The shooting is carried out in accordance with the above rules. However, vacancies are not filled.

When this shooting is not at a pre-arranged time, the shooters concerned must keep in contact with the management so as to be ready to shoot at the latest thirty minutes after the shooting proper has finished.

Art. 59. For the other places, precedence will be established according to the number of dead targets in the last stage. If the number of killed targets is the same in this stage, the last but one counts, etc. Finally, it is decided by ballot.

Art. 60. If two or more teams obtain the same score, and if no special provision has been stated in the programme, tie-shooting shall take place in accordance with Art. 58 between the teams which have equal scores in order to decide the winning team. The remaining places will be established in accordance with Art. 59.

Art. 61. Prizes of honour may be awarded for the best scores in each of the three days but the official World Championship medals are awarded in accordance with the rules

Art. 62. In international championships to which a technical representative has been delegated, this representative must, in agreement with the management, discuss arrangements, make suggestions with regard to the drawing of lots, etc. He must also take over the jury's duties, until the latter have been nominated.

Art. 63. The shooting range must be open for practice shooting at least three days before the first day of the competition. The same type of targets must be used for practice as those used for the competition.

Art. 64. If the organizing committee has not announced otherwise in the programme, it is forbidden to shoot for practice on the competition range between its stages.

Olympic Trap

1. General

1.1 These rules are part of the General and Special Technical Rules of the UIT and apply to all clay-target shooting disciplines, trap and skeet.

1.2 Every shooter, team official and competition official must be familiar with the UIT rules and must ensure that these rules are enforced.

2. *Safety*

2.1 UIT rules state only specific safety requirements which are required by the UIT for use in UIT championships. Necessary and special safety regulations for ranges differ from country to country. For this reason, only basic details are stated within the framework of these rules. The safety of a shooting range depends to a large extent on local conditions and additional safety rules may be established by the organizing committee.

The organizing committee must know the principles of range safety and take the necessary steps to apply them. The organizing committee bears the responsibility for safety.

2.2 The safety of shooters, range officials and spectators requires continued and careful attention to firearms handling and caution in moving about the range. Self-discipline is necessary on the part of all. Where such self-discipline is lacking, it is the duty of shooters and team officials to assist in such enforcement.

2.3 In the interest of safety, a jury member or a range official may stop the shooting at any time. Shooters and team officials are obliged to notify them immediately of any situation that may be dangerous, or which may cause an accident.

2.4 No one, except an equipment inspector, referee or jury member may pick up a shooter's equipment without permission.

2.5 To ensure safety, all shotguns must be handled with maximum care at all times.

(a) Shotguns may be loaded only on the shooting station and only after the command or signal to load or start firing is given.

(b) After the last shot, the shooter must ascertain before leaving the shooting station, and have the referee verify, that there are no cartridges in the chamber or magazine.

(c) Sighting exercises are permitted, but only with the permission of the referee and only on the shooting station or in a designated area. The handling of guns is not permitted when operating personnel are forward of the firing line.

(d) All shotguns must be kept unloaded except on the shooting station after the command or signal to load or start firing is given.

2.6 When the command or signal to cease fire or unload is given, shooting must stop immediately. All shooters must unload their shotguns and make them safe. Shooting may only be resumed at the appropriate command or signal.

2.7 The referee or other appropriate range officials are responsible for giving the commands to start firing, to cease fire, to unload and any others that are necessary. The referee must also ascertain that the commands are obeyed and that shotguns are handled safely. Any shooter who handles a loaded gun after the cease fire command has been given, without the permission of the referee, may be disqualified.

2.8 Ear protection: all shooters and other persons in the immediate vicinity of the firing lines are urged to wear ear-plugs, ear-muffs or other similar ear protection.

2.9 Eye protection: all shooters are urged to wear shatterproof shooting glasses or similar eye protection.

3. *Range and Target Standards*

Detailed specifications for shotgun ranges (skeet and trap) and clay targets can be found in the general technical rules.

4. *Equipment*

4.1 General: all devices, ammunition, or equipment which are not mentioned in these rules, or which are contrary to the spirit of the UIT regulations and rules, are not allowed. The jury has the right to examine the shooter's ammunition and arms at any time. Team leaders are held equally responsible for their team member's use of equipment in accordance with these rules.

4.2 Guns: all types of shotguns, including semi-automatics, may be used provided their calibre does not exceed 12 gauge. Guns smaller than 12 gauge may be used.

(a) Slings or straps on guns are prohibited.

(b) Guns with magazines must have the magazine blocked so that it is not possible to put more than one cartridge in the magazine at one time.

(c) Changing guns or functioning parts of a gun is not permitted between stations of the same round unless the referee declares a malfunction which cannot be repaired quickly (*see* Rule 8.4).

4.3 Personal attire: it is the responsbility of the shooter to appear at the shooting station dressed in a dignified manner for a public event.

4.4 Compensators or other devices which serve like purposes are prohibited on all guns in UIT trap shooting.

4.5 Olympic Trap: before shooting, the length of the cartridge must not exceed standard specifications of 70mm. Shot load must not exceed 28 grams. Pellets must be only spherical in shape, made of lead or lead alloy and not larger than 2.5mm diameter. Shot may be plated. Black powder, tracer, incendiary or other speciality-type cartridges are prohibited.

The referee or jury member may remove an unfired cartridge from a shooter's gun for inspection.

5. Competition Officials

5.1 The referee.

(a) The shooting must be conducted by a referee with wide experience in clay-target shooting and a thorough knowledge of guns. His main function is to make immediate decisions regarding dead or lost targets and to give a distinct signal for all lost targets. The referee must also make decisions on disabled guns or malfunctions.

(b) The referee must be assisted by three assistant referees who are usually appointed in rotation by the chief referee from among the shooters and preferably from those who have fired in the previous squad.

(c) All shooters must serve in this function.

(d) If a shooter has been designated as an assistant referee and fails to present himself, to give a plausible reason for refusing to serve or to provide an acceptable substitute, he must be penalized by the deduction of one target from his final result for each refusal. Subsequent refusals may result in disqualification from the competition.

(e) The main function of an assistant referee is to watch each target thrown and to give,

immediately after a shot, a signal if he considers a target lost. He must observe carefully whether the target is broken before the shot is fired.

(f) One of the assistant referees must be placed at each side of the range in such a position that he can observe the whole shooting area. The third assistant referee must be positioned near the score board to ensure that the score-keeper is posting the results correctly for each shot.

5.2 The referee must make an immediate decision whether targets are dead or lost, whether a repeat target is to be thrown, whether there are irregular targets, or whether there are other deviations from the rules. If possible he must call 'No Bird' or give some other signal before the shooter fires. Irregular targets require an immediate and very accurate decision by the referee.

5.3 A target declared 'No Bird' by the referee must always be repeated whether or not the shooter has hit it (*see* Rules 6.16–6.17).

5.4 The referee must always make the final decision himself. If any assistant referee is in disagreement, it is his duty to advise the referee by lifting an arm or otherwise attracting his attention. The referee must then arrive at a final decision.

5.5 In doubtful cases the referee must consult the assistant referees before making a final decision.

5.6 The referee's decision may be appealed in matters concerning interpretation and application of the rules. The referee's decisions are final and no appeals are permitted in matters concerning dead, lost or irregular targets.

5.7 The referee and the assistant referees, under the jury's control, are responsible for the application of the safety rules and for the correct conduct of the competition.

6. Shooting Event Procedures and Competition Rules

6.1 The shooter must stand with both feet within the limits of the shooting station.

6.2 A regular target is any unbroken target called by the shooter and released according to these rules.

6.3 A broken target is any target which is not

whole in accordance with section 3, general technical rules. The shooter receiving a broken target must repeat the shot on a regular target regardless of whether he hit or missed it.

6.4 Disciplinary regulations:

(a) It is the responsibility of the shooter to be present on the proper station at the proper time with all necessary equipment and ammunition and ready to shoot.

(b) If a shooter is not present at the station when his name is called, the referee must have the shooter's name called loudly three times within one minute. If the shooter does not appear within the three calls, the referee must declare him absent loudly. From that moment the shooter declared absent must not be allowed to join the squad and shooting will begin without him. He may be permitted to shoot the missed round at a time and on the field decided by the chief referee but the shooter must be penalized with a deduction of three targets. The penalty must be deducted from the results of the make-up round.

(c) A competitor declared absent must present himself before the chief referee to obtain permission to shoot the missed round before it is finished. Failure to do so must result in his disqualification from the competition.

(d) If a shooter uses guns or ammunition which are not in accordance with Rule 4.4, all shots fired with such guns or such ammunition are to be scored as misses. If the jury finds that the shooter has committed such a violation deliberately, it may disqualify him from the competition. If, however, the jury finds that the shooter could not reasonably be aware of the fault and that he, through the fault, has attained no essential advantage, the jury may decide to ignore the fault.

(e) If the shooter leaves his squad for one of the reasons cited in Rule 8.3 or for other reasons specified in these rules, a penalty of one target must be imposed for each interruption and he must be permitted to shoot the remaining targets at a later time.

(f) If the shooter leaves his squad without one of the reasons cited in these rules, or without a reason accepted and approved by the referee, all remaining targets of the round must be scored as misses ('Lost'). Unsportsmanlike conduct or serious violations of the rules of conduct can cause the shooter to be disqualified from the competition by the decision of the jury (*see* Rule 6.4(c)).

(g) all other violations which are not included in the preceding Rules or specific rules, must be a cause for a warning to be given the shooter who has committed them for the first time. Subsequent occurrences during a 25-target round must be penalized by one target each.

(h) Unsportsmanlike conduct or deliberate attempts to evade the spirit of these rules may incur a warning, a penalty, or disqualification from the competition based on the decision of the jury or the jury of appeal.

6.5 Conduct of a round of trap: squads which are composed of less than six official shooters in the drawing of lots should be filled with proficient shooters for the duration of the championship. These auxiliary shooters should have scores posted in the normal manner on the large board and the official score-card in order to provide continuity. However, their names or nationality must not be listed in any document.

6.6 When the shooter is ready to fire, he must raise the gun to his shoulder and call crisply and loudly 'Pull' or some other signal or command, after which the target must be thrown at once. The shooter must not leave his station before the shooter at his right side has fired a regular target, except when the shooter has completed shooting on Station 5. In the latter case, he must proceed immediately to Station 1, being careful that he does not disturb the shooters who are on the line as he passes by.

6.7 A shooter must position himself, load his gun and call for his target within fifteen seconds after the shooter to his left has fired at a regular target or after the referee has given the signal to start firing. In case of non-compliance with this time limit, the penalties provided in Rule 6.4(g) will be applied.

6.8 Before the beginning of a round and after each subsequent setting of the traps, a trial target must be thrown from each trap in sequence.

6.9 If the shooter is interrupted within a round for more than five minutes because of technical malfunction that is not the fault of the shooter, the squad must be allowed to view one

Preparing for a low-house target at ISU Skeet.

regular target from each machine in the group on which the interruption took place before starting the competition again.

6.10   Targets must be thrown for each shooter according to these rules:

(a)   Two shots may be fired at each target.

(b)   At the beginning of each round the first five shooters must take positions on Stations 1 to 5, the sixth shooter must remain behind Station 1 ready to move in as soon as Shooter No. 1 has shot. After Shooter No. 1 has fired at a regular target, he must prepare to move to Station 2 as soon as the shooter on that station has fired and so on. When the shooter on Station 5 has fired, he must immediately move around the rear of the firing line and return to Station 1, continuing the rotation until each shooter has fired twenty-five targets. No shooter having shot on one station shall proceed toward the next station in such a way as to interfere with another shooter or officials.

(c)   When the shooter has called for his target it must be released immediately allowing only for human reaction time to press a button whether the release is manual, electrical or mechanical.

(d)   If a target is not thrown immediately after the shooter's call, the shooter may refuse the target by removing his gun from his shoulder.

6.11   The trap event.

Target distance, angles and elevations: traps must be set before the beginning of the competition. The settings must be examined, approved and sealed by the clay target jury.

(a)   New settings must be made only when all shooters have completed fifty targets on that range. The traps must be set according to the specifications provided.

The height of the target path above the level of the trap-house roof at 10 metres forward of the throwing point must be between 1.5 metres and 3.5 metres.

A tolerance of 0.5 metres (a minimum of 1 metre and a maximum of 4 metres) is permitted.

After the traps have been adjusted and approved by the jury, one trial target must be thrown from each machine in sequence. These trial targets may be observed by the shooters. All shooters, trainers and team officials are prohibited from entering the trap pits after the jury has examined and approved the trap settings.

6.12   Irregular targets: any target flying along a path other than that specified in angle, elevation and distance must be considered irregular.

6.13   A target is declared 'Dead' when it is thrown and hit according to the rules and at least one visible piece is broken from it.

6.14   A target is declared 'Lost' when:

(a)   it is not hit during its flight;

(c)   it is only 'dusted' and no visible piece is broken from it;

(c)   the shooter does not fire at a regular target for which he has called;

(d)   the shooter is not able to fire his gun because he has not released the safety, has forgotten to load or has failed to cock his gun;

(e)   the first shot is a miss and the shooter fails to fire his second shot because he forgot to place a second cartridge in the gun, to release the stop on the magazine on a semi-automatic shotgun, or because the safety has slipped to the 'safe' position by recoil of the first shot;

(f)   a malfunction of the gun or the ammunition occurs and the shooter opens the gun or touches the safety before the referee has examined the gun;

(g)   it is the third subsequent malfunction of the gun or the ammunition for the same shooter in a 25-target round;

(h)   the shooter does not fire for any other reason.

6.15   A 'No Bird' target is one which is not thrown according to these rules. The 'No Bird' decision is always the referee's responsibility.

6.16   A target declared 'No Bird' by the referee must always be repeated whether the shooter has fired or not and whether he has hit or missed the target.

6.17   In case of a 'No Bird' target, a new target must be thrown from the same trap that has caused the 'No Bird.' The shooter may not refuse it even if he considers that it was thrown from another machine in the same group.

Exception: If a shooter has shot at a correct target and has a misfire or malfunction on his second shot, the target must be repeated from the same trap.

6.18 After a 'No Bird', another target must be thrown according to the following conditions:

6.19 another target must be thrown (whether or not the shooter has fired) when:

(a) a broken target emerges or an irregular target emerges;

(b) the target is thrown by a machine in another group;

(c) two or more targets are thrown simultaneously from machines in the same group or from different groups on the same range;

(d) the target is of a colour manifestly different from that of the others used in the competition;

(e) a shooter shoots out of turn.

6.20 Another target may be thrown (provided the shooter has fired) when:

(a) the target is thrown before the shooter calls;

(b) the target is not thrown immediately after the call and the shooter refuses it by removing his gun from his shoulder;

(c) the shooter's first shot misfires due to a malfunction of either gun or ammunition and he does not fire the second shot. If the second shot was fired the result must be scored.

Note: In the case of a third or subsequent malfunction, rather than 'No Bird', the target is declared 'Lost'.

6.21 Another target may be thrown (even if the shooter has fired) when:

(a) the first shot is a miss and the shooter's second shot misfires due to malfunction of either the gun or the ammunition except under Rules 6.14(a)–6.14(g). In this case, the target must be a miss for the first shot and hit only for the second shot. If the target is hit with the first shot, it must be declared 'Lost'.

Note: A shooter using a double-barrel gun with a single trigger must declare to the referee, before the beginning of the competition, which barrel he is going to fire first. If he fails to make this declaration, it must be assumed that the lower barrel is being fired first in the over-and-under guns and the right-hand barrel is first in side-by-side guns;

(b) the shooter has been visibly disturbed;

(c) another shooter has fired at his target;

(d) the referee is unable, for any reason whatsoever, to rule whether the target is dead, 'Lost' or 'No Bird'. In this case, before making a final decision, the referee must consult the assistant referee;

(e) when the shooter's turn comes and he discharges a shot involuntarily before he has called for his target. Accidental discharges may be cause for penalty or disqualification from a competition for unsafe gun handling.

If after the first shot, the target is thrown and the shooter fires at the target with the second, the result must be scored.

6.22 'No Bird' must not be declared when two shots are discharged simultaneously or in rapid succession. The result must be scored according to the outcome of the two shots.

7. Pre-Match Administration (Squadding)

7.1 Individual seniors (men and women): the event consists of 200 targets for UIT championships shot in eight rounds of twenty-five targets each. They may be shot in two days of 100 targets each day or in three days with seventy-five + seventy-five + fifty targets. Under extremely crowded conditions, an event may be scheduled for four days of fifty targets per day.

7.2 After 150 targets, a portion of the shooters up to a maximum of 50 per cent with lowest scores, may be eliminated from the remaining rounds of the individual event. If sufficient details on elimination standards are not given in the programme, the elimination procedure must be decided by the jury before the start of the event.

7.3 Team senior (men and women): teams consist of three shooters per team. The team event must be decided by the totals of the results of the individual scores of the three team members over the first 150 targets (first 6 rounds).

7.4 Shooting order – squadding:

(a) A squad normally consists of six shooters except when the draw does not permit an even distribution.

(b) Whenever possible in UIT championships, the draw must be made so that the shooters of each country are distributed in such a way that no squad will contain more than one shooter from one country.

(c) Drawings are made by the jury on a pre-determined day which must be announced to the team officials of the participating nations so they can be present. Attendance at the draw by the team officials is optional.

(d) The jury may proceed with the draw whether team officials are present at the announced time or not.

7.5 It is the shooter's responsibility to be on the proper station at the right time with sufficient ammunition and the necessary equipment.

7.6 Once shooting has been started it must continue according to the programme without interruption, except for mechanical breakdown. Only the chief referee may interrupt the shooting with the jury's approval in the event of heavy rain or a storm.

Malfunctions

8.1 In the event of misfire due to any reason, the shooter must remain standing with the gun pointed to the target flight area without opening the gun or touching the safety until the referee has inspected the gun.

8.2 Disabled shotguns and malfunctions:

(a) A shotgun must be considered disabled if:
   (i) it cannot be fired safely;
   (ii) it does not ignite the powder charge;
   (iii) it fails to eject due to a mechanical defect.

(b) The following are not considered malfunctions:
   (i) Faulty manipulation by the shooter.
   (ii) Failure to place the cartridge in the proper chamber of the gun.
   (iii) Empty shells in the chamber or chambers.

(c) Decisions on disabled shotguns or malfunctions must be made by the referee.

8.3 Ammunition. The following are considered ammunition malfunctions when the firing-pin indentation is clearly noticeable and:
(a) only the primer fires;
(b) the powder charge is omitted;
(c) the powder charge is not ignited;
(d) the components of the load remain in the barrel.

Decisions on ammunition malfunctions must be made by the referee. Cartridges of the wrong size are not considered defective ammunition.

8.4 Actions after malfunctions are declared.

(a) If the referee decides that the disabled gun or malfunctioning of gun or ammunition is not the fault of the shooter, and that the gun is not repairable quickly enough, the shooter may use another approved gun if it can be obtained within three minutes after the gun has been declared disabled.

(b) Or, the shooter may, after obtaining the permission of the referee, leave the squad and finish the remaining targets of the round at a time determined by the referee.

(c) If the shooter leaves the field for more than three minutes, the penalties in Rule 6.4 must apply.

(d) If the gun is repaired before the end of the round, the shooter may be allowed to rejoin his squad with the permission of the referee.

8.5 Number of malfunctions allowed.

(a) The shooter is allowed a maximum of two malfunctions per round whether or not he has changed his gun or ammunition.

(b) Any regular target on which any additional malfunction of gun or ammunition occurs will be declared 'Lost', whether or not the shooter attempted to fire.

9. *Rules of Conduct for Shooters and Team Officials*

Rules of conduct deal with discipline on the shooting station, infringement of rules or safety regulations and disqualification.

9.1 It is the responsibility of the team leader to be thoroughly familiar with the rules and the programme. Team leaders are further responsible for seeing that shooters present themselves at their shooting stations at the proper time with proper equipment. If a team is small and does not have a non-competing leader, one of the shooters should be designated team leader before the competition begins.

9.2 Coaching is not allowed in UIT competitions while the shooter is in the shooting area. Trainers and coaches are not permitted inside the shooting areas.

9.3 Rules for handling shotguns:

(a) All guns, even when empty, must be handled with the greatest of care.

(b) Conventional double-barrel guns must be carried with the breech open, and semi-automatic guns with breech-bolt open and the muzzle pointed in a safe direction, up or down towards the ground.

(c) Guns not in use must be placed in a gun-stand.

(d) It is forbidden to touch or handle another shooter's gun without the owner's permission.

9.4 Shooting or sighting:

(a) Sighting is permitted only on the shooting station or in a designated area.

(b) Shots may be fired only when it is the shooter's turn and the target has been thrown.

(c) Sighting or shooting at another shooter's targets is forbidden.

(d) Deliberately sighting or shooting at live birds or other animals is prohibited.

(e) Test firing of guns may be done on the range prior to the beginning of a round only with the permission of the referee.

9.5 Cartridges must not be placed in any part of the gun until the shooter is standing on his shooting station, facing the traps with the gun pointed toward the target flight area and after the referee has given permission to load.

9.6 The shooter must not turn from the shooting station before his gun is opened. When an irregular target is thrown or shooting is interrupted, the gun must be opened. No gun may be closed until the order to continue has been given.

9.7 Shooters must not cause any interruption of the shooting other than those allowed in these rules and must restrict their conversations to calling for their targets, 'Ready'; protesting, or answering the questions of the referee.

9.8 The shooter must not close his gun before the next shooter on his left side is ready to fire.

9.9 All guns must be carried open when moving between Stations 1 and 5 and must be carried open and unloaded when moving from Station 5 to Station 1.

11. Scoring Procedures

11.1 For individual events: for each shooter, the results of each round must be entered legibly on official score-sheets. At the end of the event the total of targets hit by an individual shooter must be entered and scores must be ranked in decreasing order of merit.

11.2 For team events: scores of each team member must be entered according to the method indicated in Rule 10.1.

Team scores must be ranked in decreasing order of merit according to the total of targets hit by all the members of each team.

11.3 Scoring: scoring is done officially on each field for each round of twenty-five targets.

In UIT championship events, scores must be kept on each field by two separate persons. One must maintain a permanent official score-card, the second person must maintain a large score-board for the benefit of the shooters and spectators. The person entering scores on the official score-card must be positioned at the rear of the firing line near the referee. Each scorer must mark his card or board independently, based on the decisions given by the referee. At the conclusion of each round the results must be compared and any discrepancy must be resolved before the official card is delivered to the classification office. The scores shown on the large score-board must prevail if there are discrepancies. It is the duty of the assistant referee nearest the large score-board to ensure that the scorer is posting the referee's decisions correctly.

11.4 When a round has been completed and the results have been compared and read aloud, the referee and each shooter must sign or initial the score-sheet so that it can be returned to the classification office quickly.

Failure to sign the sheet before it leaves the field eliminates the right to protest scores other than scores erroneously posted from the score-sheets.

11.5 The classification office. When the shot-gun events are part of a larger competition, such as the Olympics or World Shooting Championships, the classification work is the responsibility of the classification office. It is the duty of the classification office to:

(a) prepare a list of shooters and assign a number of each;

(b) assist the jury in the drawing of lots to squad the shooters;

Note the concentration as this competitor prepares to shoot a target below him.

(c) prepare score-cards for each squad;

(d) ensure that the proper score-card is with the correct squad on the correct field;

(e) receive and verify results and total the targets hit at the end of a round;

(f) tabulate scores and post-preliminary scores on the public bulletin board immediately. Total the official scores daily within the shortest possible time:

(g) prepare a preliminary results bulletin for distribution to the press and team officials each day;

(h) prepare and publish a final results bulletin immediately after the completion of an event and at the close of any applicable protest period;

(i) send ten copies of the official results and any other reports to the UIT Secretariat within thirty days after the completion of the events.

Tie-Breaking

12.1 Individual ties. If two or more shooters have equal scores, ties for the first three places in the event must be decided by a shoot-off in rounds of twenty-five targets up to a maximum of three tie-breaking rounds. If the tie is not broken after three rounds, the shooters will be ranked equally.

All shoot-off rounds must be conducted according to these rules. In the trap event, the shooting stations that are not occupied by shooters must not be taken by other shooters as otherwise provided in Rule 6.5. If the shoot-off time is not arranged in advance, the shooters involved must keep in touch with the jury, whether personally or through their team leader, in order to be ready to shoot when the shoot-off is scheduled. Shoot-offs should be scheduled within a maximum time limit of thirty minutes after regular shooting is completed.

(a) Individual fourth- through to tenth-place ties must be broken by the scores of the last round of twenty-five targets. In case of an unbroken tie, the round before the last round must count, etc. If the results of all rounds are equal, ties must be decided by counting from the last target forward until a zero is found and the shooter with the most hits in succession must be given the higher place.

(b) Individual scores ranking eleventh place and below must be listed in equal rank in alphabetical order by family name in the Latin alphabet with an appropriate number of spaces left unnumbered before the next placing is numbered. Within the tie score, ranking of the names will be alphabetical.

12.2 If two or more teams have the same scores, ranking must be decided by the combined score of the team members in the last round of twenty-five targets, then by the next to the last round, etc. until the tie is broken.

13. Protests and Appeals

13.1 If a shooter disagrees with a referee's decision, a protest may be initiated by raising an arm and saying 'Protest'. The referee must then interrupt the shooting temporarily and after hearing the opinions of the assistant referees, make his decision. There is no appeal against a decision on a hit or missed target and the referee's decision is final. Retrieving clay targets from the field to determine whether or not they have been hit is not allowed.

13.2 If the shooter or team leader is not satisfied with the final decision of the referee they must not delay the shooting. They may make a notation on the score-card that the shooter is continuing under protest. This protest must be resolved by the shotgun jury.

13.3 Protests to the shotgun jury may be made verbally or in writing. Either must be accompanied by a fee. A written protest must be submitted before a jury decision can be appealed to the jury of appeal. If the protest is upheld the fee will be returned. If the protest is denied the fee will be turned over to the UIT with the written protest and the jury's decision.

13.4 If the shooter or team leader is dissatisfied with the decision of the shotgun jury, he may appeal, writing to the jury of appeal.

English Skeet

Target and Trajectories

Art. 1. In calm conditions both traps shall be set so that one target shall emerge from a trap-house (high house) at a point 91cm beyond the station marker 1 (measured along the base, chord extended) and 3.05m above the level of Station 1. The other target shall emerge from a trap-house (low house) at a point 91cm beyond station marker 7 (measured along the base, chord extended) and 76cms from the base, chord extended (measured on the side of the target crossing point) and 1.07m above the level of Station 7. The targets shall fly a distance of 50 to 52 metres after passing within 45cm of a point 4.57 metres above the ground known as the target crossing point. Where the referee is satisfied that variation in target trajectory is such that the equity of the competition cannot be maintained, he may ask the jury to reset the targets.

Art. 2. Targets to be used shall comply with ISU rules.

Art. 3. Regular target: One which having been set as in rule 1, appears instantly when the shooter calls.

Art. 4. An irregular target:

(a) An unbroken target which has not conformed to the definition of a regular target.

(b) Two targets thrown simultaneously in singles.

(c) Targets thrown broken. Under no circumstances shall the result of firing at a broken target be counted.

Art. 5. Regular doubles: a regular target thrown from each trap-house simultaneously.

Art. 6. Irregular doubles:

(a) Either or both targets of a double are thrown as irregular targets.

(b) Only one target is thrown.

Organization of Competitions

Art. 7. Shooting is normally conducted in squads of five competitors. If it becomes necessary, squads of less than five members may be formed but squads of more than six must be avoided for control and safety reasons.

Art. 8. The targets will be shot in the following sequences:

Station 1: two singles and a double.
Station 2: two singles and a double.
Station 3: two singles.
Station 4: two singles and a double (the shooter must nominate the first target of the double).

Station 5: two singles.
Station 6: two singles and a double.
Station 7: two singles and a double. Optional or repeat target – the first target missed or a single from either high or low on Station 7. This shall be scored as the twenty-fifth shot.

Art. 9. The first target to be shot at in doubles on Stations 1 and 2 will be the high house and, on Stations 6 and 7, it shall be the low house.

Art. 10. Each shooter shall complete his shooting on one stand before leaving that stand.

Art. 11. At the beginning of each round, when the squad is assembled at Station 1, they shall be entitled to observe one regular target from each trap-house. A competitor may also ask to have one regular target thrown after each irregular target, except when the irregular target was fired at.

Art. 12. If a shooter is not present when his squad is called the referee must call the name three times loudly within the period of one minute. If he does not appear then, the shooting shall commence without him. In order to be eligible to shoot in that round, a late member must arrive in time to shoot his first bird before the No. 1 man of his squad has taken his position at Station 2.

Art. 13. If a breakdown occurs to a trap during the shooting, the referee will decide if the shooting will be continued on another layout or on the same layout after the breakdown has been repaired. The squad shall be entitled to observe one regular target from each trap-house before shooting continues.

Referees and Jury

Art. 14. The shooting shall be conducted by a referee with wide experience in skeet shooting. His main function is to make immediate decisions regarding dead or lost targets and he is to give a distinct signal for all lost targets.

Art. 15. The referee shall make an immediate decision whether a repeat target is to be thrown due to an irregular target or some other reason. If possible he shall call 'No Bird' before the shooter has fired his first shot.

Art. 16. A jury shall be formed consisting of five members representative of the competing shooters, who shall elect a chairman.

Art. 17.   It is the duty of the jury:
(a)   to ascertain that the ranges and targets thrown conform to regulations;
(b)   to see, during the shooting, that the rules are adhered to and to examine the guns, ammunition and targets by random tests or other suitable procedures;
(c)   to make decisions in connection with technical defects or other disturbances in the shooting, if these are not made by the referee;
(d)   to deal with protests;
(e)   to make decisions regarding penalty if a shooter does not adhere to the regulations or conducts himself in an unsportsmanlike manner;
(f)   to agree upon a plan so that at least two members of the jury are always present on the ranges.

Guns and Ammunition

Art. 18.   All types of guns, including semi-automatics, 12 gauge and smaller may be used for shooting. No handicap will be given to competitors using a gun of a calibre smaller than 12 gauge.
Art. 19.   The length of the cartridge, before being fired, is not to exceed 70mm (except for .410 cartridges). The shot load not to exceed 28 grams or size larger than 2mm diameter (No. 9 shot English). Cartridges must be of normal loading; no internal changes may be made. Each round of skeet will be completed with one type only, those being the ones with which the round was started. Different loads or shot sizes will not be used within the round. (The referee may at any time remove an unfired cartridge from a shooter's gun for inspection.) Black powder and trace cartridges are forbidden.
Art. 20.   When a gun fails to function and the referee on inspection finds that it is disabled in such manner as to render it not quickly repairable, and that this has not been caused by the shooter himself, the shooter should have the option of using another gun if one can be secured without delay, or dropping out of the squad and finishing the remaining shots at a later time when a vacancy occurs and the referee gives his permission. If his gun is repaired before the end of the round, the shooter may be permitted to rejoin the squad providing the referee gives his permission.

In other cases of malfunction of either guns or ammunition, which result in the shot not leaving the gun (providing this is not the fault of the shooter), he has the choice of changing his gun or continuing with the same one. A competitor is allowed to repeat targets (malfunction of gun and ammunition combined) during each round of twenty-five targets, one for each malfunction whether he has changed his gun or not.

A shot will be considered a misfire (valid malfunction) if there is not detonation after the primer has been struck.

Should the shooter not release the trigger sufficiently to fire the record cartridge of a souble or to cause (automatic) fan-firing, this will be considered the fault of the shooter and will not entitle him to a repeat target.

Shooting Rules

Art. 21.   One shot only may be fired at each target during its flight within the shooting bounds — an area 40.2 metres in front of the trap-house from which the target is thrown.
Art. 22.   Shooting position: standing with both feet entirely within the boundary of the shooting stand. Gun position optional.
Art. 23.   When the shooter is ready to shoot, he calls loudly 'Pull' or some other verbal command after which the target shall be thrown instantly.

Dead and Lost Targets

Art. 24.   A target is declared 'Dead' when it is completely destroyed or a visible piece falls as a result of being fired upon according to these regulations.

The referee shall be the sole judge of a 'Dead' or 'Lost' target.
Art. 25.   The target shall be declared 'Lost' if:
(a)   the target is not broken or it is hit outside the shooting boundary;
(b)   the target is only dusted;
(c)   the shooter has been unable to fire because the safety catch has not been released, or because the gun has not been properly loaded or closed;

(d) the third or subsequent malfunction of gun or ammunition occurs to a shooter in a 25-bird round;

(e) when firing a double, a competitor is unable to fire his second shot because he has failed to load a second cartridge; or he has incorrectly set a semi-automatic gun; or the recoil from the first shot has applied the safety catch; or the second round is discharged by the recoil from the first shot; or for any other reason whatsoever attributable to the shooter;

(f) during doubles, the second shot does not leave because the competitor using single trigger has not released it sufficiently after the first shot;

(g) after a misfire or malfunction, a competitor touches the safety catch or opens the gun before the referee has inspected it;

(h) the shot is not fired due to some other reason which does not entitle the shooter to a repeat target;

(i) the doubles are fired in inverse order both targets shall be scored 'Lost'.

'No Bird'

Art. 26. Under the following circumstances, 'No Bird' shall he declared and another target thrown whether or not the competitor has fired:

(a) The target breaks on throwing.

(b) The target is thrown from the wrong trap-house.

(c) Two targets are thrown simultaneously in singles.

(d) The target is of a colour manifestly different from that of the others used in the competition.

(e) The first target in doubles is regular and the second is irregular.

Art. 27. 'No Bird' shall be declared and another target thrown if the competitor has not fired:

(a) when the target is thrown before the shooter has called;

(b) when the target does not appear immediately;

(c) when the target flutters, has insufficient velocity or takes an irregular course on leaving the trap;

(d) when the shooter's position is not according to Rule 22 and the shooter has not been warned in the round.

No claim of irregularity shall be allowed where targets were actually fired upon and the alleged irregularity consists of deviation from the prescribed line of flight, or because of an alleged 'quick' or 'slow' pull unless the referee has distinctly called 'No Bird' prior to the firing of the shot in the event of the 'quick' pull, or prior to the emergence of the target in the event of the 'slow' pull. Otherwise, if the shooter fires, the result shall be scored.

Art. 28. In the case of a misfire or a malfunction of gun or ammunition through no fault of the shooter, 'No Bird' shall be declared and a repeat target thrown a maximum of two times for each shooter in a round of twenty-five targets regardless of whether the shooter changes his gun or not. Upon the third and succeeding malfunctions, the targets are scored as lost targets.

Art. 29. The referee may also permit a new target to be thrown if:

(a) the shooter has been visibly distracted;

(b) another shooter fires at the same target;

(c) the referee cannot for some reason decide whether the target was hit or missed.

The referee will not declare a 'No Bird' if the shooter misses a target for reasons other than those covered by the rules regarding 'No Bird'.

Art. 30. The foregoing rules may also apply to doubles and will be interpreted as follows:

(a) The double will be declared 'No Bird' and the competitor must shoot a regular double to determine the result of both shots if:

(i) the first target is regular and the second is irregular, regardless of whether the first target is dead or lost:

(ii) a malfunctioning gun or ammunition prevents the shooter from firing at the first target;

(iii) either target of the double is irregular and the shooter does not fire. If the alleged trajectory consists of a deviation from normal, insufficient initial velocity or a fast or slow pull and if both targets have been shot at, the results must be counted;

(iv) the shooter misses his first target and it collides with the second target before the shooter fires his second shot, or if the fragments from the first target break the second target before he has fired his second shot;

(v) the referee prevents the shooter from shooting his second shot because of violation of Rule 22. If the shooter has already been warned of the same violation during the same round, the result of the first shot will be recorded and the second target will be declared 'Lost'.

(b) Lost targets will be declared:

(i) upon the third and subsequent malfunction of the gun or faulty ammunition in the same round;

(ii) if the shooter (without legitimate reason) does not fire at a regular double. Both targets will be declared lost.

(iii) if the shooter (without legitimate reason) does not fire at the second target of a regular double. The result of the first target will be recorded and the second target declared lost.

(iv) if, in a regular double, the first target is lost and the second shot cannot be fired because of a malfunction of the gun or ammunition. The first target is scored 'Lost' and the double repeated to determine the result of the second shot only.

Art. 31. (a) If, in the course of shooting doubles, both shots are discharged simultaneously, the double is declared 'No Bird' and is repeated as a regular double to determine the result of both shots if the first target was hit.

If the first target is missed the target shall be scored 'Lost' and the double repeated to determine the result of the second shot only.

(b) If the shooter breaks both targets with the same shot, the double will be declared 'No Bird' and repeated. The shooter is allowed three attempts on one station. On the fourth attempt if the same situation occurs, the double will be scored 'Dead' and 'Lost'.

(c) If, in shooting at a regular double, the shooter misses the first target and accidentally hits the second target with the same shot, he will be scored 'Lost' first target and shoot again at a regular pair of doubles to determine the result of the second shot only. The shooter is allowed three attempts on one station. On the

fourth attempt, if the same situation occurs, the double will be scored 'Lost' and 'Lost'.

Art. 32. Shots will not be scored:

(a) if the shooter fires out of turn;

(b) if the shot is discharged involuntarily before the shooter has called for his target. Accidental discharges may be cause for penalty or elimination from a competition for unsafe gun handling.

Rules of Conduct

Art. 33. All guns, even when empty, shall be handled with the greatest care.

Conventional double-barrel guns are to be carried with the breech open and the muzzle in a safe direction, up or down at the ground. Straps or slings on guns are prohibited. When a shooter puts his gun aside it must be placed vertically in a gun-stand or another place intended for this purpose. It is forbidden to touch or handle another competitor's gun without the owner's specific permission.

Art. 34. Shooting and sighting may only be practised on the shooting station. Shots may only be fired when it is the shooter's turn and the target has been thrown. It is forbidden to sight or shoot at another competitor's targets. It is also forbidden to wilfully sight or shoot at live birds or animals.

Art. 35. At roll-call, before the beginning of a round, the shooter must be ready to shoot immediately and take with him sufficient ammunition and other necessary equipment.

Art. 36. No member of a squad shall advance to the shooting station until it is his turn to shoot and the previous shooter has left the shooting station. No member of the squad having shot from one station shall proceed towards the next station in such a way as to interfere with another shooter.

Art. 37. It is prohibited to place cartridges into any part of the gun before the shooter is standing on the station with the gun pointed in the direction of the target flight area and the referee has indicated that shooting may begin. During shooting of singles it is permitted to load only one cartridge in the gun at a time.

Art. 38. If the target is not thrown instantly the shooter is to denote that he refuses the target by remaining in his 'ready' position. (The referee shall be the sole judge of determining a slow or fast pull.)

Art. 39. After a shot has been fired, or after a regular target has been thrown without the shot being fired, the competitor must not turn away from the target flight area before opening his gun.

When an irregular target ('No Bird') has been thrown or the shooting interrupted, the gun shall be opened. It is not to be closed again until shooting can continue.

Art. 40. In the case of a misfire or other malfunction of gun or ammunition the shooter shall remain standing with the gun pointed to the flight area without opening the gun or touching the safety catch until the referee has inspected the gun.

Art. 41. The shooting shall be carried out without interruption. The shooter shall indicate he is ready to call for his targets or indicate a protest if necessary. The shooter shall answer any of the referee's questions.

Art. 42. The referee, under the supervision of the jury, shall see that these regulations and safety precautions are adhered to.

Protests

Art. 43. A referee shall not be interfered with or interrupted unnecessarily. Protests submitted to a member of the jury either verbally or in writing shall be accompanied by a fee to be set by the jury. If the protest is upheld by the jury then the fee shall be returned.

Art. 44. If a competitor disagrees with the referees decision regarding a shot, a protest should be initiated immediately by raising the arm and saying 'Protest' or 'Appeal'. The referee shall then interrupt the shooting and make his decision. It is not allowed to pick up a target from the field in order to find out whether it has been hit or not.

Art. 45. The referee's decision can be appealed against verbally or in writing to the jury. If the jury finds the protest justified it can give the referee directions for future decisions or appoint a new referee or alter his decision if this does not concern hits, misses or irregular targets where the referee's decision is final.

Art. 46. If the shooter is of the opinion that the score which is read aloud when the round is finished is incorrect, he should make protest verbally to the referee immediately. The referee shall then, as soon as possible, examine the score-sheet after which he shall announce his decision. If the person protesting is not satisfied with the decision, a short written protest shall be made to the jury.

Art. 47. If a competitor or official observes anything which does not conform to these rules, he must not interfere with the shooting but shall report his findings to the referee or a member of the jury. Action shall then be taken.

Penalties, etc.

Art. 48. Every competitor is obligated to acquaint himself with the rules in so far as they apply to shooters. By entering the competition he thereby agrees to submit to any penalty that may be incurred through failure to comply with the rules or with the referee's decision.

Art. 49. If the shooter uses guns or ammunition which are not in accordance with Rules 18 and 19, all shots fired with such gun or such ammunition shall be counted as misses. If the jury finds that the fault has been committed with intent, it can, in consequence hereof, exclude the shooter from the competition. If the jury finds that the shooter could not be reasonably aware of the fault and that he, through the fault, has attained no essential advantage, it can decide to approve of the shooting results, providing the fault is corrected as soon as the shooter has become aware of it.

Art. 50. If the shooter is not present after the referee has called his name and number three times, and this is not due to circumstances beyond his control, the shooter is to be fined three birds and given the opportunity to shoot the remaining targets of the round at a time to be decided. If the competitor leaves his group for one of the reasons cited in the rules, a penalty of one target shall be imposed for each interruption and he shall be permitted to shoot the remaining targets at a later time.

Art. 51. Should the jury find that a shooter delays the shooting or conducts himself in an

'*Now do exactly as I told you . . .*'

unsportsmanlike manner, it may give him a warning or fine him one bird or exclude him from the match.

Art. 52. When the jury fines a shooter one bird and the decision is not occasioned by any special target, the first dead target after the decision is made known is to be counted as 'Lost'. If the shooter has completed the day's shooting or the whole competition, one bird shall be deducted from the score of the last round.

If a shooter has been designated as an stannate referee and is late or fails to present himself or provide an acceptable substitute without delaying the squad, he shall first receive a warning in the case of being late and shall be penalized by one target by the jury if he fails to appear or provide an acceptable substitute.

Ties

Art. 53. If two or more shooters obtain equal scores, precedence for the first three places in championships (and in other competitions where this has been announced in the programme) are decided by tie-shooting in 25-bird rounds until a difference in scores occurs. The round or rounds shall be shot according to these rules in such a way, however, that the scores may consist of less than five men. Unless the tie-shooting is to be held at a pre-arranged time, the shooters involved shall keep in touch with the management so that the tie-shooting can be carried out at least thirty minutes after the shooting proper is finished.

Art. 54. For the remaining scores, the last 25-bird round is to decide precedence; thereafter, the second to last and so forth. If all stages are equal, precedence is decided by counting the last target forward until a zero is found; the shooter with most hits in succession takes precedence.

Art. 55. If two or more teams obtain the same scores, ranking will be determined by the total score of the team members in the last series of twenty-five targets and, then, next to the last series, etc., until the tie is broken.

Unfinished Competition

Art. 56. Should any competition fail to be completed due to extreme bad weather, dark-ness or major equipment failure, the competition may be curtailed or suspended.

If curtailed, the award of prizes should be decided at some point in the competition equitable with fair play. It is recommended that a proportional refund should be made to each competitor.

If suspended, it shall be announced publicly at the suspended shoot a date at and the terms under which the competition shall continue. Such dates should not be more than four weeks from the date of the original competition.

Any competitor who fails to attend on the new date set for the postponed competition shall forfeit all rights and standing in the competition. A refund of entry fee should be paid.

International Skeet

The UIT's special technical rules for International Skeet are identical in most ways to those for Olympic Trap. They vary only in the following areas, which govern shot size, gun mounting and, of course, shooting procedure.

4.4 Skeet cartridges. Before firing, the length of the cartridge must not exceed 70mm. The shot charge must not exceed 28 grams Pellets must be spherical in shape, made of lead or lead alloy. and not larger than 2.0mm in diameter.

6.5 Timer. The traps must be operated by an electrical or mechanical device which is so installed as to allow the operator (puller) to see and hear the shooters. For all UIT Championships, a timer must be used. This device must allow for the release of the targets within an indefinite period of time, varying from instant release up to a maximum three seconds after the shooter has called for his target.

The release device must be so constructed that only one button or switch must be used to release the doubles targets.

(a) Until the target appears, the competitor must stay in the 'ready' position, holding the gun with both hands so that gun butt touches the crest of the hip bone.

(b) No prolongation of the gun butt is permitted. To aid the referee in controlling the position of the gun, a mark approximately 10cm long × 2cm wide must be firmly affixed on the right side of the outer garment (left side for left-handed shooters).

(c) When the shooter is ready to shoot he must call crisply and loudly 'Pull', or some other signal or command after which the targets must be thrown within an indefinite period not to exceed three seconds.

6.6 Each squad must start shooting in the shooting order indicated by the drawing of lots. Each shooter in the squad, starting at Station 1, will shoot the targets in sequence to Station 8 according to the following:

Station 1: one single from the high house. One double, shooting the high-house target first and the low-house target second.

Station 2: two singles, shooting the high-house target first and the low-house target second. One double shooting the high-house target first and the low-house target second.

Station 3: same as Station 2.

Station 4: two singles, shooting the high-house target first and the low-house target second.

Station 5: two singles, shooting the high-house target first and the low-house target second. One double, shooting the low-house target first and the high-house target second.

Station 6: same as Station 5.

Station 7: one double, shooting the low-house target first and the high-house target second.

Station 8: one single from the high house, one single from the low house.

When the squad advances to Station 8, they must stand in their shooting order behind the referee on an imaginary line drawn between the centre of Station 8 and Station 4.

The first shooter must position himself in a normal manner on Station 8 and, after loading the gun with one cartridge only, shoot the high-house target. Then he must turn clockwise, to the right, in the direction of the target crossing point. He will position himself for the low-house, loading his gun with one cartridge only and shoot the low-house target.

He must leave the station and move to the rear of the line of shooters who must still shoot. Each shooter will do the same in succession.

6.7 Number of cartridges.

(a) On Station 1 only one cartridge may be loaded to shoot the high-house single target.

(b) On Stations 2, 3, 4, 5 and 6, two cartridges must be loaded to shoot single targets and two cartridges to shoot the doubles fired on Stations 1, 2, 3, 4, 5, 6 and 7.

(c) On Station 8 only one cartridge may be loaded to shoot at the target emerging from the high house. After firing on that target, another cartridge may be loaded for the low-house target.

(d) During single-target shooting with the gun loaded with two cartridges, the shooter must not open his gun after shooting the first of the two singles. If, inadvertently or deliberately, the shooter opens his gun, he must be warned the first time he does so in each series of twenty-five targets. The second and subsequent times, the target must be considered 'Lost'.

(e) Only on Stations 1 and 8 may the shooter raise his gun to his shoulder and sight for a few seconds, both for single and double targets and on Station 8 both for the high-house target and low-house target. After that, the shooter must return to the 'ready' position described earlier before calling for a target.

Appendix III

CLAY SHOOTING CLUBS

There are more than 700 clubs affiliated to the Clay Pigeon Shooting Association. Some of the clubs that stage regular events are listed below, region by region.

Details of forthcoming events can be obtained from the clubs concerned, or by checking the fixture lists published in the magazines listed in Appendix IV.

North Region

Allerton Bywater Colliery CPC
Allerton
Castleford
West Yorkshire

Ancholme Valley SG
Kirton-in-Lindsey
near Gainsborough
South Humberside

Batley and District GC
Birkby Brow Wood
Howden Clough
near Morley
Leeds

Bobbin Mill SG
Bobbin Mill
Scorton
near Preston
Lancashire

Bywell SG
Bywell Farm
Felton
Northumbria

Carlisle and District GC
Great Orton Airfield
Wiggonby
Carlisle

Cleveland GC
Lingdale
Cleveland

Cockermouth and District CTSA
Clints Quarry
Moota
Cockermouth
Cumbria

Cotton Dale SG
America Farm
Staxton
North Yorkshire

Deerplay CPC
Deerplay Inn
Burnley Road
Bacup
Lancashire

East Yorkshire GC
Bygot Wood
Cherry Burton
near Beverley
East Yorkshire

Hesketh GC
Guide Road
Hesketh Bank
near Preston
Lancashire

Humberside SG
Catwick Lane
Brandesburton
near Beverley
North Humberside

Knaresborough and District GC
Boroughbridge Road
Knaresborough
North Yorkshire

Knowsley GSC
Appletons Farm
Cut Lane
East Lancashire Road
Kirkby
Liverpool

North of England CTC
Tinker Lane
Rufforth
York

North Wolds GC
Uncleby Wold
Kirby Underdale
York

North Yorkshire SG
Felixkirk
near Thirsk
North Yorkshire

Penrith and District GC
Bowscar
Penrith
Cumbria

Steve Smith SG
Dinington
Northumberland

Teesdale GC
Bail Hill
Mickleton
Teesdale
County Durham

Wensleydale GC
Victoria Arms
Worton
near Aysgarth
North Yorkshire

Westhoughton GC
Reeves House Farm
Westhoughton
near Bolton
Lancashire

East Midlands Region

Bagworth Miners CPC
Bagworth Colliery
Station Road
Bagworth
Leicestershire

Fenland GC
Washbrook Farm
Doddington
near March
Cambridgeshire

Flitwick GC
Folly Farm
Maulden Road
Flitwick
Bedfordshire

High Lodge SS
Henham Park
Blytheburgh
Suffolk

Lakenheath Rod and GC
RAF Lakenheath
Brandon
Suffolk

Leicestershire Wildfowlers' Association
Kibworth Shooting Ground
Harborough Road
Leicestershire

Market Harborough and District SC
Airfield Farm
Market Harborough
Leicestershire

167

Mepal CTC
Mepal Airfield
Sutton
near Ely
Cambridgeshire

Mid-Norfolk SG
Deighton Hills
Taverham
Norwich
Norfolk

Northampton SG
Sywell Range
Kettering Road
Northampton

Nottingham and District GC
Nine miles north of Nottingham on A614.

Orston GC
Bottesford Lane
Orston
Nottinghamshire

RAF Bentwaters Rod and GC
RAF Station
Bentwaters
Woodbridge
Suffolk

Stilehollow SS
Off A616 between Ollerton and Budby,
Nottinghamshire

Sutton Bridge GC
Chalk Lane
Sutton Bridge
Spalding
Lincolnshire

Thurlaston GC
Normanton Dairy Farm
Thurlaston
Leicestershire

Vale of Belvoir GC
Bottesford Lane
Orston
Nottinghamshire

West Midlands Region

Basford SG
Basford
near Leek
Staffordshire

Blakelow CSC
Higher Blakelow Farm
off A537 Macclesfield-Buxton Road
Macclesfield
Cheshire

Bridgnorth and District GC
Naboth's Vineyard
Shipley Common
Pattingham
near Wolverhampton

Brown Edge SG
Broad Lane
Brown Edge
Stoke-on-Trent
Staffordshire

Catton Hall SG
Catton Hall
Bradley Lane
Frodsham
Cheshire

Charlesworth SS
Tanyard Farm
Mossy Lea
Old Glossop
Derbyshire

Chatcombe Estate SS
Chatcombe Estate
Chatcombe
Coberley
Cheltenham
Gloucestershire

Doveridge Sporting Club
Eaton Hall
Doveridge
Derbyshire

Edge Hill SG
Nadbury House
Camp Lane
Ratley
Warwickshire

Garlands SG
Raddle Farm
Edingale
Tamworth
Staffordshire

Grange SG
Hewell Park
near Redditch
Worcestershire

Grouse SG
Chunal Road
Glossop
Derbyshire

Hayfield GC
Kinder Bank
above Sportsman Inn
Kinder Road
Hayfield
Derbyshire

Hereford GC
Haywood Shooting Ground
Haywood
Hereford

Leek and District GC
Westwood Shooting Ground
Leek
Staffordshire

Lyme SG
Lyme Park
Disley
Stockport
Cheshire

Millride CSC
Millride Centre
Hill Farm
Hilton Park
Essington
Wolverhampton

Quarnford SG
Off A53 Buxton–Leek Road, four miles from
Buxton

West Midlands SG
Hodnet
near Market Drayton
Shropshire

Worsley Grange SG
Botany Bay Wood
Grange Road
Worsley
Lancashire

Yeaveley SG
Yeaveley
Ashbourne
Derbyshire

Yoxall and District GC
Kingstanding Airfield
Needwood
Burton-on-Trent
Staffordshire

South-West Region

Abbo's CTC
Allet
off A30 near Zelah
Cornwall

Apsley SG
Apsley Estate
Andover
Hampshire

Blagdon Valley GC
Middle Ellick Farm
Blagdon
Somerset

Camelford and District GC
Helsbury Quarry
Michaelstow
near Camelford
Cornwall

Cheddar Valley SG
Draycott Moor
Draycott
Cheddar
Somerset

County GC
Lower Lake
Upton Cross
Liskeard
Cornwall

Dorset SS
Wardon Hill
near Evershot
Dorchester
Dorset

Fareham GC
Titchfield Lane
Funtley
near Fareham
Hampshire

Fieldsman SG
Tadpole Farm
Lady Lane
Blunsdon
Swindon
Wiltshire

Frome Valley CSG
Doreys Farm
East Holme
Wareham
Dorset

Gosport and Fareham SGC
Cherque Farm
Shoot Lane
Lee-on-Solent
Hampshire

Lains SG
Lains Farm
Quarley
near Andover
Hampshire

Long Sutton GC
Long Sutton
near Odiham
Hampshire

Royal County of Berkshire SG
Tomb Farm
Upper Basildon
Berkshire

Stour Valley SG
Newton Farm
Sturminster Newton
Dorset

Urchfont CPC
Redhorn Hill
near Urchfont
Wiltshire

West Cornwall SG
Ludgvan
Penzance
Cornwall

South-East Region

Ashdown CPC
Lower Flitteridge Wood
Fletching
West Sussex

Chalk Pit CPC
Alfriston
Polegate
East Sussex

Christmas Common SG
Churchill Shooting Ground
Christmas Common
Wallington
Oxford

Hoggs Farm
Harlow Common
Essex

Lea Valley SS
Bramfield Road
Hertfordshire

Lower Lodge SG
The Haven
Billingshurst
Sussex

Mid-Kent SS
Langley
Maidstone
Kent

West Kent SS
Elm Court Estate
Lidsing Chatham
Kent

Windmill CSC
Great Mill
Lower Assendon
Henley-on-Thames
Oxon

Woodchurch GC
Boulder Wall Farm
Dungeness Road
Lydd
Kent

Appendix IV

MAGAZINES

There are a number of magazines available which cover the international, domestic and local clay-shooting scene. Those listed are especially recommended.

Clay Shooting, bi-monthly from third Friday of February.
Pull!, monthly, free to CPSA members.

BOOKS

Bentley, P., *Clay Target Shooting*, A & C Black (1987)

Cradock, C., *Cradock on Shotguns*, B. T. Batsford Ltd (1989)

Reynolds, M., *Shooting Made Easy*, The Crowood Press (1986)

Smith, A. J., *Sporting Clays*, Argus Books (1989)

Thomas, G., *Shotguns and Cartridges for Game and Clays*, fourth edition, A & C Black (1987)

Shooting Gazette, bi-monthly.
Shooting Times, weekly.
Sporting Gun, monthly.

If you are a member of the CPSA, the excellent *Pull!* will be delivered to your home. Of the rest, *Clay Shooting* and *Sporting Gun* offer the most comprehensive coverage of competitive clay shooting at all levels as well as detailed fixture lists and results.

Useful Addresses

ASSOCIATIONS

British Association for Shooting and Conservation (BASC)
Marford Mill
Rossett
Clwyd
LL12 0HL

Clay Pigeon Shooting Associastion (CPSA)
107 Epping New Road
Buckhurst Hill
Essex
IG9 5TQ

Federation de Tir aux Armes Sportives de Chasse (FITASC)
10 Rue de Lisbonne
75008 Paris
France.

PROOF HOUSES

The Birmingham Gun Barrel Proof House
Banbury Street
Birmingham
B5 5RH

The Gunmakers Company
48 Commercial Road
London
EL1 1LP

Index